Contents

This history is dedicated to George Cooke CBE, who was instrumental in bringing both the Education Management Information Exchange and the Education Policy Information Centre (now EURYDICE) to the NFER, in gratitude for the many years he devoted to supporting and promoting these information services among the educational community in this country and in Europe.

nfer

The First Fifty Years
1946–1996

Jeffrey L Griffiths

nfer

National Foundation for Educational Research

The photographs in this book are reproduced with permission from the following:

University of London Institute of Education Archives, pages 3, 5, 20, 25, 30, 98

London Metropolitan Archives, page 7

Jeffrey L. Griffiths, pages 11, 109, 122

Wendy Crees, page 16

Dr Joyce M. Morris, page 32

NFER Archives (Tim Wright), pages 36, 57, 77, 85, 93, 95, 101, 104, 118, 127

Val Hincks, pages 59, 104

George Cooke, page 80

Christopher Hill Photography, page 113

Published in May 2003
by the National Foundation for Educational Research,
The Mere, Upton Park, Slough, Berkshire SL1 2DQ

Preface

The fiftieth anniversary of the National Foundation for Educational Research, celebrated in 1996, was an occasion of pride for those associated with the organisation. It was decided to commission this history to record the Foundation's evolution and growth over that half century, which would update a brief account that had been written at the time of its Silver Jubilee. Established in the immediate aftermath of the Second World War, through the vision of a few individuals, the NFER has survived and flourished amidst a host of changes that have followed its founding. In serving the local authorities of England and Wales, and their schools, the Foundation has experienced with them the multitude of developments that have shaped education in a half century of profound change. Those who have led and served the Foundation have needed to be sensitive to the aspirations of politicians, at local and national levels, who have moulded the developing pattern of education, as well as to the needs of the practitioners who have had to implement these changes. The NFER has constantly striven to maintain its independence and objectivity amidst the pressures of these decades, and to develop its expertise in order to meet new challenges.

All quotations in the text, unless otherwise indicated, are taken from the NFER's Annual Reports contemporary to the events described. These Reports provided the principal source for much of this work and dictated the chronological arrangement of this history. The interpretation of events is that of the author, as is the responsibility for any errors and omissions. The time period in the main body of the text extends to 1996, the year when the Foundation celebrated its Golden Jubilee.

Acknowledgements

I am grateful to many people for the help they have given in the preparation of this history. Most especially, I thank the Director of the NFER, Dr Seamus Hegarty, for the opportunity to tell this tale and for patiently awaiting the outcome of my researches. I appreciate the assistance that was given by various members of the NFER's Board who were interviewed in the course of preparing this history. NFER Assistant Directors, Dr Judy Bradley, Dr Sheila Stoney and Chris Whetton, provided valuable guidance to me from their long, collective knowledge of the organisation. Nick Tester undertook the initial research, and conducted a number of interviews, which greatly assisted me. Alfred Yates's account of the first 25 years of the NFER, and his other writings, were invaluable. Sir Edward Britton, George Cooke, David May-Bowles, Dr Joyce Morris, Dr Ray Sumner, and Professor William Wall made important contributions to this history from their long knowledge of, and involvement with, the NFER. I appreciate the support I was given at the outset by Ralph Tabberer, who launched me on this history, and by Wendy Tury, who helped me see it through to its final publication stage. I am very grateful for the help given by Janet May-Bowles, Pauline Benefield, Katie Longfield and Ellie Stephens, in the NFER library. Others in the Foundation who have been of particular assistance to me include Jennie Campion, Adrian Clark, Stephanie Cornell, Laura Davis, Mary Hargreaves, Dr John Harland, Gill Holt, Alison Lawson, Jane Lever, Dr Julie Nelson, Robat Powell and David Upton. I wish to record too my gratitude for the support and help given to me by my colleagues in the Education Management Information Exchange, especially to Richard Downing, who produced the Index to this work, as well as to Valerie Gee and Alison Riley.

Outside of the Foundation, I especially wish to record my gratitude to Professor Richard Aldrich, whose centenary history of the University of London Institute of Education appeared shortly before the publication of this work and which was of great value for its illuminating accounts of individuals and developments common to both organisations. I am indebted also to Diana Guthrie in the Institute's Library, who gave me access to *The Sir Fred Clarke Papers* (Clarke, n.d.), which proved a rich source of information on the early period of the Foundation's life, and Sarah Aitchison, who kindly gained permission to reproduce a number of the photographs from the Institute's archives.

I also thank the Carnegie Corporation of New York for information about the archives they hold relating to the International Examinations Enquiry and their grant to the Foundation; Sue Harris of Birmingham City Council's Local Studies and History Service, who provided information about both the NFER's first Director and an early Chairman of the Executive committee; and Jane Parkin of the National Children's Bureau, who directed my attention to articles about the origins of that organisation.

On a personal level, I thank Marylyn Griffiths for providing me with unwavering support during the numerous weekends when I was preparing this publication.

I am indebted as well to the many I have not had the opportunity to name but who have, none the less, helped to shape my understanding of the NFER. These include that large band of former colleagues I have known in my time at the NFER whose anecdotes – the best of which were often recounted in their farewell speeches – have convinced me that the Foundation is, and has been, a special place in which to work.

The preparation of this history took far longer than envisaged and I can only endorse the sentiments of Dr George Jeffery, Director of the University of London Institute of Education between 1945 and 1957, and the second Chairman of the Foundation's Executive Committee, that 'the writing of history is a slow business and cannot be hurried even at the dictates of directors' (Aldrich, 2002:1).

Jeff Griffiths
May 2003

Foreword

Educational research has been our business since the 1940s. We owe an immense debt of gratitude to those farsighted individuals who, at a time when Britain faced major economic as well as educational challenges, had the vision to establish a national research capacity in education. From modest beginnings in 1946 we have grown to a point where we are one of the largest concentrations of research expertise in education anywhere in the world. We have a strong national and international reputation, and are an important feature of the educational landscape.

It has not been all plain sailing, however. Educational research has had a long struggle to be taken seriously and secure the resources necessary to conduct studies to a high standard and communicate findings to teachers and education policy makers.

It is particularly gratifying therefore to be able to present this history at a time when there is growing understanding of the role of educational research in furthering educational reform. Having been saying for more than half a century that research is essential to informed practice and sound policy making, we are naturally pleased that others have come round to our way of thinking! We have not been alone in flying the flag for educational research, but we have made a unique contribution through the volume of research we have conducted, our efforts to collate information about educational research nationally and our commitment to communicating research findings to wider audiences.

Jeff Griffiths has done a superb job in building on Alfred Yates' account of the Foundation's first 25 years. Much happened in the intervening period, and the Foundation's activities and staffing increased greatly. This was a period of very great change in the world of education more generally. The dynamic context of educational reform which characterised the 1980s and 1990s inevitably affected the Foundation, creating pressures but also significant opportunities. As this history demonstrates, the Foundation flourished during this period. While maintaining our independence, we reinforced our position as an authoritative source of educational measurement, research and evaluation data, and information on educational issues.

Those many people who have been associated with the Foundation over the years will find much of interest here, while a more general readership will learn of our involvement in the key educational developments of recent decades. We are proud of our contribution to education in Britain and beyond, and I have very great pleasure in introducing this history of our first 50 years.

Seamus Hegarty
Director
May 2003

Chapter 1

The Birth of the Foundation
1931–1946

The year adopted for the start of the Foundation is 1946 but it is an organisation which experienced a protracted birth. As the historian of the NFER's first 25 years had stated, a case can be made for each of the years from 1945–1948 as the key year in the emergence of the NFER (Yates, 1971:4). Events leading up to the institution of the NFER had begun in 1931 when the Carnegie Corporation[1] of New York undertook to fund the International Examinations Enquiry. A number of UK researchers were invited to join with others in France, Germany and Switzerland to take part in the Enquiry, which was intended to check the reliability and validity of formal public examinations (Hartog and Rhodes, 1936). That part of the Enquiry which was undertaken in England and Wales proceeded under a committee whose chairman was Sir Michael Sadler (see below). This vast investigation was, in its turn, to whet the appetite not only of the researchers but also educational administrators and teachers in this country to have an organisation which could perform similar surveys on a regular basis.

Up to this period, little systematic research had been undertaken in this country. In 1894 an Office of Special Enquiries and Reports, responsible to the Board of Education, had been established with permission from the Treasury to spend annually no more than £2,400. Its Director, Michael Sadler, voiced many arguments that would be recognised by later generations of researchers when he wrote in 1903:

In the present ferment of opinion as to national education, the work of a well equipped educational intelligence office might do much to provide unity of educational effort, understanding of the needs of different types of schools and a clearness of educational aims. In the past, much public money has been wasted through failure to make a careful study of educational methods and problems before embarking on schemes entailing large expenditure. It is probable that great savings would be effected by the supply of timely information on many educational subjects for the consideration of those locally interested in the supply and management of schools. The aim of the writers of such reports should be to give practical help to educational workers, without being narrowly statistical or doctrinaire ... It should be their aim to disentangle what is valuable from what is obsolete or antiquated in our English educational traditions, and to preserve all that is good in our present educational arrangements...

(Taylor, 1973:3–4)

Sadler also stressed the need for independence in a manner that bodies like the NFER, which were to follow the pioneering work of the Office of Special Enquiries and Reports, would applaud:

In order that the scientific work of educational enquiry may be searching and fruitful, it must be intellectually independent. Those engaged in it must be free to state what they believe to be true, apart from preconsiderations as to what may at the time be thought administratively convenient.

(Taylor, 1973:4–5)

Some of the earliest chairs of education had been set up in Scottish universities (Edinburgh and St Andrews, 1876) and it was Scotland too that led the way in 1928 with the founding of the Scottish Council for Research in Education (SCRE), which was to prove a model for the NFER. But Scotland, in its turn, had followed in the footsteps of continental and transatlantic pioneers:

Educational research as it is now understood appeared first, not in Scotland, but abroad in Europe and in the United States of America when educationalists realised that the quantitative methods of the exact sciences could be applied with profit to the investigation and solution of many educational problems. There is little evidence that these trends of thought had reached Scotland before the close of the First World War.

(Craigie, 1972:2)

In 1932, the London Day Training College (LDTC), in whose establishment the Fabian Socialist Sidney Webb had been a prime mover, was transformed into the Institute of Education, which then came under the aegis of the University of London. It was a change in role and status that had been well earned through the quality of the work that had been pioneered at the LDTC. Its Director, Percy Nunn, had imagined that the Institute might become 'a centre of educational thought, inquiry and training for the British Commonwealth' (Aldrich, 2002:84). 'One of the key elements envisaged for the new Institute of Education as established in 1932', writes Richard Aldrich, its historian, 'was the creation of a Bureau of Educational Enquiries and Research. Such a Bureau was seen as exercising a co-ordinating function in respect of educational research throughout the country' (Aldrich 2002:125). The first steps towards the establishment of that Bureau, which became the

Sir Fred Clarke, 'A Founder and Faithful Friend' of the NFER

NFER, were taken in the late 1930s when two of those educationalists who had been members of the committee involved with the International Examinations Enquiry in this country, Sir Fred Clarke and Sir Philip Hartog, were instrumental in obtaining from the Carnegie Corporation a grant of $10,000 to support educational research on condition that an equal amount was raised in this country. The minutes of the first meeting of the Advisory Council of the Educational Research Fund on 13 January 1943, quoting a statement made at that meeting by Sir Philip himself, actually record that 'The Carnegie Corporation of New York approached Sir Philip and offered a grant as a sign of appreciation for the work that had been done [by the English Committee of the International Examinations Enquiry]' (Clarke, n. d.).

Sir Fred Clarke was appointed Professor of Education at Hartley College, Southampton, when aged just 25: he later went on to fill professorial chairs of education at the Universities of Cape Town, and McGill in Montreal. Appointed Professor of Education and the Director of the Institute of Education in the University of London in 1936, he served in this office up until 1945. Fred Clarke, described by his predecessor at the Institute, Sir Percy Nunn, as 'the wisest man he knew' (Aldrich, 2002:91), was a person of strong Christian faith and who held a high regard for English cultural traditions (Curtis, 1953:532). Sir Philip Hartog had been appointed the Academic Registrar of the

University of London in 1903: he later went on to play an important role in the Indian sub-continent as a member of the Public Service Commission there and as Vice-Chancellor of Dacca University. He was also responsible for directing the English section of the Carnegie International Examinations Enquiry. They have been described as 'men of such unusual stature that they were able both to keep their heads in the clouds and their feet firmly on the ground. They recognised that the fulfilment of vision calls for hard cash and they set about looking for some' (Yates, 1971:3). The Carnegie Corporation met their request to contribute to a research fund and it was agreed that the University of London Institute of Education should administer this fund, so beginning a strong association that has lasted for many years between the Institute and the Foundation.

Considerable delay was caused by the Second World War, although by the end of 1940 a group had been set up within the Board of Education to plan the post-war reform of the education system (Maclure, 2000:xix). Discussions about new legislative measures had, vitally for the future Foundation, included the proposal that the Ministry of Education and the LEAs should be given specific powers to fund research to help improve the quality and range of educational provision. But it was not until 1942, with growing optimism about the outcome of hostilities together with the prospect of legislation that would result in the Education Act 1944, that the campaign to create a research institute was seriously resumed.

A condition agreed upon by the parties in receipt of the Carnegie grant was that, in expending the money on educational research, the London Institute of Education would take the advice of a body representative of the main interests concerned with education in England and Wales. In November 1942, the minutes of an executive meeting of the Association of Education Committees (AEC) reported that the Institute had drawn up a proposed structure and had set about the composition of an Advisory Council – to which the AEC was itself invited to nominate a representative – to administer research activities financed from the funds donated by the Carnegie Corporation. (It has been calculated that the Carnegie grant of $10,000 would, in today's values, have represented a sum of around £40,000.)

This Advisory Council first met in January 1943 under the chairmanship of Professor Fred Clarke, who was knighted in that same month for his services to education. It was decided to set up a fully representative and autonomous body that should be known as the Foundation for Educational Research and whose Advisory Council would begin examining a variety of research techniques and planning schemes of research. This work was to be undertaken with the close cooperation of the University of London Institute of Education and among the members of that Advisory Council were three of the Institute's academic staff, Professor Herbert Hamley, Dr Charlotte Fleming and Dr J.W. Jenkins, who acted as its Secretary.

A memorandum of 1944 records that:

The Foundation owes its origin to a strongly-expressed conviction revealed by representatives of English education, who when consulted by the Institute of Education on a scheme for administering certain funds that had been made available for research, urged the immediate setting-up of a permanent organisation. The purpose of this organisation would be to explore new ways of undertaking systematic educational research in this country, and at the same time to introduce more co-ordination and effectiveness into whatever research was being done. Some sort of national organisation seems to be desirable that would not stultify or supplant existing university departments of education and training colleges, that would exercise a tactful control over the wide field of necessary research. It would also supplement what was being done in these other institutions by undertaking research itself, including that which could be carried out best by an organisation which was not in any way hindered by training duties and other limitations from bringing its endeavours to a speedy and successful conclusion.

Professor Herbert Hamley, an early advocate of the NFER

(Clarke, n. d.)

Constitutionally, the Foundation for Educational Research was defined as 'an independent institution with its own Advisory Council working in association with the Institute of Education, and under the tutelage of the University of London which receives and administers its funds'. The Higher Degrees and Research Staff of the Institute of Education under Professor Hamley were stated in this memorandum to be working for the Foundation under agreed terms. Active work was said to have begun on 1 March 1944, although this movement to found a research organisation was said to have been 'developing for a number of years, and in fact several abortive attempts have been made in the past to establish a working organisation... [which had] received an impetus from the circumstances of the war and the passage of the Education Bill through the House of Commons'.

The memorandum went on to state that invitations in the educational press to help this new organisation with its investigations had received 'a very generous response' from over 300 separate institutions, from university to nursery school level, which would potentially involve 700 persons. It records that: 'Naturally our programme of work has been fixed by the urgency of the times' and enumerated eight issues in which it was engaged, *viz*. selection for secondary education, with 93 local education authorities having provided details of their schemes; a continuous school record booklet; improved tests of intellectual capacity; a suitable curriculum for the secondary modern school; and, likewise, for technical education; 'the collection of sociological and psychological evidence of the influence of evacuation upon individual character and ability' (presumably, this referred to the mass evacuation of children that had taken place from parts of Britain thought vulnerable to aerial bombing during the Second World War);[2] improvements in rural education 'by means of an experimental rural school'; and a 'possible common curriculum for pupils between the ages of 11 and 13' (Clarke, n. d.).

The first paid employee taken on by the fledgling organisation was Mr Lea Perkins, a former President of the Incorporated Association of Assistant Masters, appointed in March 1944 as Secretary to the Foundation. In May that same year, a further appointment was made with Dr Jane Darroch employed as a Psychological Assistant. One of Perkins' pressing concerns was to meet the terms of the Carnegie Corporation grant by raising matching funds in this country. By the end of 1944 rather more than £6,300 had been raised, with the National Union of Teachers providing a substantial grant of £2,000 and the Leverhulme Trust giving £1,000.[3] A little over £300 was also received from the Dr H. G. Stead Memorial Fund. Further donations were obtained through the generosity of the other bodies representing the teachers, i.e. the Joint Four Secondary Teachers' Associations (£300), the Association of Teachers in Training Colleges and Departments of Education (£100); the Association of Teachers in Technical Institutions (£75); and the Association of Head Teachers (£52.10s). These precise figures were cited in the Humble Petition to the Privy Council for incorporation by Royal Charter (see page 9) (Clarke, n. d.).

A financial estimate was provided to the Advisory Council which was said to represent 'the cost of a very moderate minimum scheme of activities, which would not last more than two years' and which pointed out that some of the work being done on its behalf was voluntary and unremunerated. It was also declared that 'We badly need suitable housing accommodation, furniture and research equipment. At present we occupy one room in the basement and one in the annex of 42, Portman Square [the wartime home of the Institute of Education]. We also require a considerably larger staff, and that staff should be much better paid for the important work they are undertaking. The high prices of material for research is another charge which is likely to increase' (Clarke, n. d.). In this manner, the infant organisation began taking its first hesitant steps.

42 Portman Square, London

A letter from R. A. Butler, the wartime Minister of Education and the architect of the momentous Education Act of 1944, to Sir Fred Clarke in November 1944, puts forward his tentative ideas for the Foundation for Educational Research, praising him for 'establishing a very promising plant' which he hoped 'would become rooted on a somewhat wider basis than at present'. Butler wrote that he saw a picture evolving of 'a National Institute for Educational Research which would take its place in the education service and be supported by the whole service. I conceive that every Local Education Authority would be a member and every University, together with the Teachers' Associations and other appropriate educational bodies.' The financing of it should, he suggested, be by corporate membership as well as by individual Associates' annual subscriptions – 'I have no doubt that large numbers of teachers would be glad to have such a personal contact' – and he also indicated that 'this Ministry would be ready to extend appropriate assistance' (Clarke, n. d.).

The Minister's ideas were duly acted upon and, in December 1945, a conference was summoned which consisted of representatives of the local education authorities, teachers' associations, the universities and the members of the Advisory Council of the Foundation for Educational Research. The conference was presented with proposals for the institution of a National Foundation for Educational Research in England and Wales which was to operate on a non-profit making basis with two types of membership, corporate and individual. The former was open to all the universities, LEAs and teachers' associations, and other educational organisations approved by the governing body of the Foundation: individual membership was open to all persons concerned with education. The Council of the Foundation, as its governing body, was to be fully representative of the corporate membership and to include representatives of the Ministry of Education and co-opted individual members. The defined aims and functions of the Foundation were very wide and included liaising with other national research bodies, such as the Scottish Council for Research in Education; acting as a liaison body with any international bodies for research in education; performing the role of an advisory body available to the Ministry of Education; and providing information and an interchange of ideas on educational questions, especially relating to research. As Yates commented in his Silver Jubilee history, 'Thus the distinctive character of the Foundation – as a research organisation serving the interests of the local authorities, the major teachers' associations and the universities – was prescribed from the outset' (Yates, 1971:3).

The delegate conference, after considering these proposals, resolved to transform the existing Foundation into a national body and their first resolution was to invite the Minister of Education to become the President of the National Foundation for Educational Research. While Alfred Yates' history of the Foundation on the occasion of its Silver Jubilee lists George Tomlinson,[4] an ex-Chairman of the Association of Education Committees who became the Labour government's Minister of Education in February 1947, as the first of the NFER's Presidents, the minutes of the Interim Executive Committee (Clarke, n. d.) state that this honour was held by Miss Ellen Wilkinson,[5] 'whose interest in our work was very real, though ill health prevented her coming to our meetings', who was the Minister of Education from August 1945 and who died in office in 1947. Pending incorporation, the University of London was asked to continue to administer the Foundation's funds but the new body assumed responsibility for its staff, premises and the researches then in progress.

The secretariat had by then transferred to 17 Manchester Square, also in London's West End, and additional staff appointments included a 'Computer' – a person in this case, not an item of technology – engaged at a wage of £300 per annum, and a 16-year-old Junior Clerk who was to be employed at 'the usual salary in these days of £2.10s a week (including bonus)'. Even in its infancy, the new body was anxious to spread the news of its emergence internationally and the Secretary, Lea Perkins, circulated details of the Foundation to a number of overseas countries – Australia, Canada, New Zealand and the USA. It was reported that news of the Foundation, sent in January 1944, had reached New South Wales by July of that year, a reminder of the problems of communication in those war-torn years.

The 1945 conference appointed an Interim Executive, representative of all the interests, under the chairmanship of Sir Fred Clarke, with Mr Will Griffith, a former President of the National Union of Teachers, as Vice-Chairman, and Dr William Alexander, General Secretary of the Association of Education Committees, appointed as the first Treasurer. Among other responsibilities, the Interim Executive was to arrange to petition the Privy Council for a Royal Charter for the incorporation of the Foundation. Additionally, the conference resolved that, in order to deal adequately with research problems distinctive of educational life in Wales, a Welsh section should be instituted: the Minister of Education had also expressly requested that such a body should be constituted because of research problems that had recently arisen in connection with school organisation in Wales. An Interim Welsh Committee was set up under Will Griffith which included representatives of the Welsh local education authorities (and Monmouthshire, this authority having at that time an ambiguous border status), university colleges and teachers' organisations, with observers from the Ministry of Education. The Foundation's involvement in the educational life of Wales was therefore established from its earliest days. Minutes of the Advisory Council of the Foundation for Educational Research in March 1945 also record that the Ministry of Education for Northern Ireland had requested that 'in some suitable way it might become linked with the Foundation in its researches' (Clarke, n. d.).

A formal resolution was passed at a meeting of the Association of Education Committees in 1946 welcoming the founding of the NFER and recommending that all LEAs should support this new research body. Such support was forthcoming and the Foundation's first Annual Report in 1947 stated that all the universities (with one exception), 140 out of 147 local education authorities, and all the national teachers' associations had become corporate members and had provided financial aid. The names of over 30 individual members, including a future Director of the Foundation, Stephen Wiseman, were also recorded in the first Annual Report for the period ending on 31 March 1947. The LEAs agreed a funding levy of one farthing (1/4d) per child in full-time education in their authorities, while the teachers' associations agreed to a subscription level of £8 per 1,000 members. On the basis of such financial support, the Foundation's Finance and General Purposes Committee calculated that the total income for 1947 was likely to amount to £9,728. With the Ministry of Education proving 'most sympathetic and encouraging' and many influential figures setting their signatures to a *Petition for A Royal Charter of Incorporation*, there was a justified air of optimism about the Foundation's first Annual Report.

The most important appointment still to be filled at the beginning of 1947 was the post of the first Director of the Foundation. Four applicants were invited to interview at the beginning of the year but no appointment was made. At a subsequent meeting of the Interim Executive it was decided to offer the post to Sir Peter David Innes, the recently retired Chief Education Officer in Birmingham, who accepted in February that year.

Innes, a Scot, appears to have been somewhat of a 'Renaissance man' on the evidence of his academic achievements. He was educated at the Perth Academy, and the universities of Edinburgh, Cambridge, and Heidelberg. Having first graduated in classics, he was later to gain a Doctor of Science degree and also held qualifications in music. Innes became an Assistant Professor and then the Head of the Physics Department at Heriot Watt College in Edinburgh. He subsequently entered education administration as Principal Assistant to the Education Officer of the London County Council in 1912, a post in which he was mainly concerned with technology and the work of continuation and evening schools. In 1919, Innes moved to Birmingham to take up the post of Chief Education Officer, in which office he was to serve until March 1946. He was widely known in that city as 'Doctor P. D.', after his Christian names, until he was knighted in the 1944 Birthday Honours List.

Innes played a pivotal role in the changes that shaped one of Britain's major cities in a period that lasted from the close of the First World War to the end of the Second World War, during which time there were extensive changes to Birmingham's education system and a great expansion of the city's housing estates. Sir Peter had also served during his long and distinguished career as President of the Association for Directors and Secretaries for Education, and had been a member of the Executive of the Association of Education Committees. In addition, he had sat on a host of other influential bodies concerned with education, including the Burnham Committee and the University Grants

Committee. Five of the staff who served under Sir Peter at Birmingham had themselves become Chief Education Officers. The Chairman of the Birmingham Education Committee at the time of Innes' retirement, Alderman Sir Wilfrid Martineau, would also later play his part in shaping the Foundation's future as Chairman of the Foundation's Executive Committee.

The Foundation had acquired as its first Director someone well versed in local authority administration and politics and who had also achieved a national profile: Innes was thus superbly qualified to rally the local education authorities in support of the new body. As well as gaining a Director at the helm, another change of premises took place in December 1946. This time, it was a move to accommodation that the Foundation could at last call its own home. A 999-year lease was purchased for £9,500 on a 20-room house at 79 Wimpole Street, in the West End of London, the price of this property being provided by a generous loan from the National Union of Teachers. Such a property was bought with a view to future expansion but, initially, the Foundation was able to let the second and third floors to the National Foundation for Adult Education and the National Council for Visual Aids in Education, boosting its income with the £600 annual rental obtained from these tenants. Although this building was later to reveal its limitations, it was another positive step for the NFER to have acquired its own sizeable property in central London.

The NFER's first headquarters, 79 Wimpole Street, London

The recruitment of suitably qualified staff was a matter of deep concern to the new research organisation. As early as 1944, Professor Hamley had warned the Advisory Council that 'there were not many with the right scientific attainments and research experience in education' (Clarke, n. d.) and the Foundation's second Annual Report highlighted this issue with the warning that 'having regard to the nature, the wide scope of its operations, and the importance of its projects, it [the Foundation] will not undertake research unless it has available to deal with any particular problem persons with first class qualifications and ability and with essential research experience. As is well known, such persons are at present not easily found.' This Annual Report went on to suggest that the universities and LEAs might offer their staff a mutually advantageous secondment to the Foundation to undertake periods of full-time research. This question of recruiting suitably qualified research staff was to be a perennial problem for the Foundation and an issue which, in due time, would lead the NFER to become a 'nursery' in which many of the country's leading educational researchers would learn their craft.

While necessarily occupied with creating the structures in which to conduct research, the Interim Executive Committee did not neglect the prosecution of some major research in these early years. The first enquiry undertaken by the Foundation was into the cumulative records of school pupils, leading to the production of a standardised record card to document a child's development during schooling. Versions were produced for the infant, primary and secondary stages and by 1947 over 400,000 had already been sold, with 34 LEAs using one or more of the three types of record. A similar record card was produced for schools in Wales, with £25 paid for 'the services of an expert translator' for a version in Welsh. The Foundation was not, however, lacking in its critics. While these record cards achieved high sales figures, they were not well received by all as they required many teacher hours to complete. Mr E. W. Woodhead, the County Education Officer for Kent, who would become the Foundation's Treasurer in 1950, 'once publicly expressed the view that the NFER's record card was of doubtful value as an instrument of educational guidance but extremely serviceable if one's purpose was to stuff a mattress' (Yates, 1971:6).

Research was also taking place at that time into an appropriate analysis of intelligence, work reported as having proceeded for three years by 1947, with the testing of 10,000 children planned after the initial pilot. Other work in hand included research into rural education; into interview examinations – with assistance from the Civil Service and the three Armed Services,[6] all of which had done considerable work in this area in the preceding few years – and into children with cerebral palsy and visual impairment.

The late Dr J. W. Jenkins of the London Institute of Education had bequeathed sufficient material for a non-verbal test of mental ability which the Foundation was able to sell over some years in great numbers to the financial benefit of his widow. It was reported that 42,000 copies had been sold by 1947 and a further 5,000 had been produced in Arabic for the Sudan and other Arabic-speaking countries. Not all these early endeavours flourished, however, and 'an enquiry into the respective merits of Greek and Latin as the fundamental basis of the classical type of education' had to be abandoned after a year or so of abortive effort as the results 'were of a somewhat tentative and inconclusive nature'.

The Foundation was also consulted at this time by the Ministry of Education under Grant Regulations, 1945 (4) Educational Research, about the award of grants to other bodies, and the NFER was asked to take on the supervision of two such research projects, into museum education and practical and craft work in schools.

International contacts spread, with the first Annual Report recording that there had been communications conducted with representatives of research organisations not only in the Dominion (*sic*) countries, but also Czechoslovakia, the West Indies, and various States of the USA. It also recorded a long list of overseas visitors to the Foundation's offices from places as far flung as Bogota and Bahrain, as well as a visiting party of representatives from the Chinese Embassy in Paris.

Nearer to home, not every local education authority was happy with the agreed financial formula for supporting this new research body: the thrifty councillors of the County Borough of Blackpool had to be informed by the Foundation that their offer to pay three guineas (£3.15), instead of their assessed subscription of £22, would not be acceptable.

Notes

[1] The Carnegie Corporation of New York was created in 1911 by Andrew Carnegie, the Scottish-born steel magnate and philanthropist, to promote 'the advancement and diffusion of knowledge and understanding'. Under Carnegie's will, a proportion of grants could be used for this purpose in countries that were, or had been, members of the British Commonwealth.

[2] Small-scale evacuations of women and children had been carried out at the height of the Munich Crisis in September 1938 but the real evacuation began in September 1939. The government had planned to evacuate about 3,500,000 people but in fact only 1,500,000 made use of the official scheme.

[3] The Leverhulme Trust was established in 1925 under the Will of the first Lord Leverhulme, the entrepreneur and philanthropist. In the late 19th century, William Hesketh Lever had established Lever Brothers, which, in turn, became a cornerstone of Unilever, a major multinational company.

[4] 'George Tomlinson... had left school at 12, becoming a weaver and a trade union official...one of his claims to fame as an educationist was as an education committee chairman campaigning for the provision of boots for needy school children in the 1930s' (Maclure, 2000:1).

[5]   'The first post-War Education Minister, Ellen Wilkinson, had a well-established reputation within the labour movement and was the first state-educated head of the Education department' (Aldrich *et al.*, 2000:113). 'Red' Ellen Wilkinson, the MP for Jarrow, organised the 1936 Jarrow Crusade march of the unemployed to London. She was instrumental in persuading Parliament to pass the 1946 School Milk Act that gave free milk to all British schoolchildren.

[6]   Up until 1997, the Ministry of Defence appointed one representative on the Council: observers from the individual branches of the Armed Services also attended meetings of the NFER's Council.

Chapter 2

Taking Control
1947–1950

It was in 1947 that the Foundation really took control of its own destiny. From 1 April that year the NFER became an entirely separate and self-governing body which was no longer subject to the administrative control of the University of London under which it had been set up. Lest there be any doubt about the fact that the Foundation was a progeny of this parent body, the first Annual Report concluded with a 'special tribute to the University of London and the Institute of Education, under whose aegis the original Foundation was born' with Sir Fred Clarke, Professor Herbert Hamley and Dr George Jeffery of the Institute singled out for particular thanks for their individual contributions in launching the new research organisation.

Life at 79 Wimpole Street had its own particular character for the expanding number of NFER employees. According to Alfred Yates, Sir Peter Innes, the Foundation's first Director, would stand with watch in hand at the top of the first flight of stairs to monitor the arrival time of his staff (Yates, 1996:10). Concern about his staff's time-keeping was not to be Innes's only problem. In the aftermath of the Second World War, supplies of all kinds were much in demand. Furniture and equipment could only be obtained after considerable delay and obtaining vital paper proved 'a matter of peculiar difficulty', according to the second Annual Report. One can only guess at what agonising negotiations must have taken place at the time with the Government Licensing Department's bureaucracy, which found the fact that the NFER had not existed before the war, and therefore had no pre-war supply on which to calculate its rationed quota, 'an almost insoluble problem'. From the barely restrained comments on this issue, it would appear that strings had had to be pulled with the Ministry of Education to rectify this impasse.

The newly acquired building itself gave cause for concern, with a ceiling collapsing due to delayed and unsuspected war damage, together with the discovery of dangerous electrical wiring, and of dry rot in the basement. As Yates graphically described the situation: '...the staff – with cold feet, plaster in their hair and the smell of dry rot in their nostrils – were getting on with their work' (Yates, 1971:5). In these circumstances, it is unsurprising that those working in Wimpole Street were reported as having 'been greatly hampered by the almost continuous and noisy presence of workmen'. The building had been constructed as domestic premises (the caretaker and his wife still occupied a flat at the top of the house) and was not ideally suited for offices. The accumulation of many thousands of test papers stored in one upper room led to the ceiling on the floor below bowing dangerously. The men's toilets were in the basement and the office day was punctuated by the thud of feet on the staircase as male staff moved to and from these facilities. Some rooms were so cramped that colleagues could only meet up on the staircase landings. Such conditions could have their advantages too, however. Yates relates that 'We had a rather ambitious Secretary/administrator who...introduced internal memoranda and telephones. Since we all met each other twice a day and, in the intervals, could get in touch by shouting or banging on the floor, these were rarely utilised' (Yates, 1996:10).

Two later Directors of the Foundation, Professor William Wall and Dr Clare Burstall, have also told of their recollections of working at Wimpole Street. Professor Wall recounted his amusement at the stipulations in the lease obtained from the Howard de Walden Estate, which included the requirement that window curtains at the front of the building had to be of the same colour, and

Staff on the roof of 79 Wimpole Street, London

which expressly forbade the Foundation using the premises for immoral purposes. Working in Wimpole Street, near the heart of London's West End, had its compensations, nevertheless, with the attractions of the neighbouring Wigmore Hall, with its concert performances, and Oxford Street, for its shopping opportunities, as added enticements to the burgeoning number of staff. Some employees even enjoyed lunch hour sunbathing on the building's flat roof.

Beverages were served directly to people's desks by the tea lady, Mrs Jenkins, with biscuits and scones also dispensed to privileged members of the staff. In stark contrast to its noisy weekday bustle, Dr Burstall told of the eerie silence that then characterised this part of central London on the occasions when she had need to come into the offices on a weekend.

There was increasing work for a growing number of researchers to perform as the Foundation began firmly to establish itself. The first research begun by the Foundation after it became entirely independent and self-directing was on the major issue that had caused a number of the promoters of the NFER to want to set up a research body. The methods of allocation of pupils at the age of 11-plus had become of vital concern since the introduction of the tripartite organisation of secondary schooling, which allocated about 75 per cent of pupils to secondary modern schools and the rest either to grammar or to technical schools (Kogan, 1978:29). This had begun in the 1930s, and was formalised by the Education Act 1944, which provided secondary education for all and not, as before, for a selective minority after the age of 14. A conference was called of interested parties, from teachers and administrators to university experts in education and psychology, as well as officers of the Ministry of Education, to discuss what lines the investigation should take. A former member of HMI, Dr A. F. Watts, who had been Staff Inspector at the Ministry of Education with special responsibility for psychological work, was appointed a full-time research officer for this important project.

Another of the new research projects illustrated the understanding that had still to be achieved about the independence of the Foundation and its relationship with the government department with which it worked. Research had begun into rewards and punishments in schools, work undertaken at the specific request of the Ministry of Education after a debate in the House of Commons. According to an account of a meeting with Sir Peter Innes during a trip to Britain in 1948 undertaken by Kenneth Cunningham, the founding Director of the Australian Council for Educational Research, the manner in which the Foundation had been required to take on this project had been a cause of concern to its Director.

Although Innes was insistent that the foundation should be free to determine its own priorities, it had previously been stated in the House of Commons that the foundation (without prior consultation) would investigate the problem of corporal punishment, about which questions had been raised in the House. Some Ministry of Education officials believed that since the government supplied much of the foundation's income, they had the right to expect the foundation to investigate promptly any matters they referred to it.

(Williams, 1994: 303)

For the year ended 31 March 1948, the Ministry of Education gave its first grant to the Foundation, a sum of £3,500. This made a significant additional contribution to the NFER's income when compared with approximately £8,000, which it had received in subscriptions that year from all other sources, the principal sums coming from the LEAs, and then the teachers' associations. It appears from the above chance record of a visitor to the infant NFER that Ministry of Education officials had, however, still to come to terms with the independence demanded by this research body newly in receipt of government grant aid. In order to emphasise this principle, the second Annual Report contained some very pointed comments:

The Foundation welcomes these [Ministry of Education] *Grant conditions because they leave it complete freedom to carry through research which it thinks worth while in the order of priority it deems to be appropriate. This, naturally, does not mean that the Foundation may not include in its programme a research project which the Ministry feels to be important. It does mean, however, that the Foundation is not an agent of the Ministry employed to carry out an official series of researches any more than it is a research instrument of either the Universities or the Local Education Authorities.*

(NFER Annual Report, 1947–48)

Innes felt it was opportune to spell out at this early stage the ground rules under which the Foundation would work with its closest partners, which were also its principal paymasters. In doing so, the NFER's first Director had faced up to a basic dilemma for an independent research organisation, namely that those who pay the piper must not be allowed to dictate the tune.

The second Annual Report for 1947–1948 also referred to an issue which was enshrined from the very start as one of the Foundation's primary functions, namely the need to disseminate the outcome of research findings. 'There remains...the need to achieve a more general diffusion of the results of research among administrators and teachers in order that the schools may reap full benefit from the results of the great research activity now going on in this country and elsewhere, and that the results of this may be translated into school practice.'

One outcome of this objective was the start, during this period, of the compilation of a register of researches in education and psychology at British universities, a publication that has been regularly produced by the Foundation ever since.

With a number of research projects completed or nearing that stage, the Executive Committee needed to turn its attention to arrangements for the publication of their outcomes. Negotiations took place in 1948–9 which gave the Newnes Educational Publishing Company an exclusive licence for five years to print, publish and market NFER publications of any kind – books, periodicals or tests – throughout the world. Over 800,000 pupil cumulative records had now been sold and various LEAs – as well as the Malayan education authorities – were adapting the Foundation's school records to suit their own purposes.

The decision of the Privy Council in 1948 not to recommend that a Royal Charter be granted to the Foundation meant that a Constitution had to be drawn up, based on an earlier version presented to the meeting of delegates in December 1945. It was felt that this Constitution would suffice until such time as it was thought fit to resubmit a petition for a Royal Charter, an action that would never subsequently proceed, however. (Although a Royal Charter is simply another means of incorporation, it is one which conveys a certain respectability and distinction.) Without this, the Foundation had to content itself, instead, with the status of an educational charitable trust.

By this time, the Isle of Man and the Isles of Scilly education authorities had joined all (save for one) of the mainland counties and county boroughs, which gratifyingly were now corporate members supporting the Foundation.

In these early days, individuals outside the Foundation were able to apply for grants from the NFER to undertake research work themselves, although its Scrutiny Committee, which considered these applications, were not able to approve any of them and felt that there was ambiguity as to the sort of research they could support.

A new Staff section in the second Annual Report illustrates how fast the Foundation was growing. Lea Perkins, who was praised as having been indefatigable in promoting the activities of the new organisation, resigned from his part-time post as Secretary to the Foundation in the summer of 1947. The account of posts filled includes a bookkeeper, a clerical officer and a statistician, as well as a number of additional research staff. The Foundation was now beginning to attract eminently qualified persons as researchers. As well as recruiting Dr A. F. Watts from the HMI for the 11-plus study, Mr A. Pinsent MBE, a senior lecturer in education at the University College of Wales, Aberystwyth, took on the rewards and punishments study. Other researchers are named too, with their career achievements up to that date being described in the Annual Reports.

An important development was the creation of a Tests Division and the appointment of Dr Ian MacFarlane Smith, who came from Manchester University in September 1949 to lead this new department. The salary of the Officer-in-Charge of the Tests Division, as he was to be called, was set at £1,100 per annum rising by annual £50 increments to a figure of £1,250. (Dr MacFarlane Smith was to leave a generous bequest to the Foundation at the end of his life – see page 90.) Another celebrated staff member, Douglas Pidgeon, was also appointed at this time, initially joining the 11-plus study.

Sir Cyril Burt, NFER Vice-President 1948–1971

The financial position continued to be good, with a further boost of a considerably larger grant of £8,000 from the Ministry of Education for the financial year 1948–49, and the Executive Committee felt able to set aside £3,000 as its first capital fund investment.

After the Minister of Education, George Tomlinson, had accepted ('in his official capacity') the post of President of the Foundation, three Vice-Presidents were also appointed in June 1948, those nominated being Professor Sir Cyril Burt, the Professor of Psychology at University College, London (formerly Professor of Education at the London Institute of Education and who had been a member of the International Examinations Enquiry) (Aldrich, 2002:69–70); Sir Samuel Gurney-Dixon, that year's President of the Association of Education Committees and an influential figure in local government education; and Sir Frederick Mander, formerly the General Secretary of the National Union of Teachers, and who was then a Director of the Newnes Educational Publishing Company.

In November 1949, Sir Fred Clarke – one of the many knighted educationalists in the Foundation's early history – retired from the office of Chairman of the Executive Committee and was given fulsome praise for his unstinting efforts to create the Foundation. The links with the London Institute of Education continued unbroken, none the less, with Sir Fred's successor as Director of the Institute, Dr George Jeffery, also following him in the role of Chairman of the NFER's Executive Committee. Obituaries which appeared in these early Annual Reports mourned the passing of another two of the founding fathers of the NFER, Sir Philip Hartog, of whom it was stated that 'No one had a greater share in the establishment of the Foundation', and Professor Herbert Russell Hamley, Deputy Director of the London Institute of Education, who was lauded for the outstanding contribution he had made in advocating, and thereafter generously supporting, the Foundation.

After such an opportune beginning, the next few years were to present challenges, particularly of a financial nature. Warnings were already being sounded in the 1949–50 Annual Report that the current rate of expenditure could not be maintained without an increase in the Foundation's income. Developments had continued apace, nevertheless. The Tests Division began to establish itself as a unit of major importance, preparing and standardising the various types of educational and psychological tests required by the LEAs as well as providing an information service on all matters relating to tests. The Wimpole Street office accommodation benefited from improvements, but the lack of a library was regarded as a serious omission in the light of the many requests for information the Foundation received. The first two publications appeared in 1950: the first was a register of researches in education and psychology in the universities of Great Britain, compiled by Mrs A. M. Blackwell, a senior lecturer in education at King's College, London, and described as 'a concrete symbol of the Foundation's desire to help in the co-ordination and facilitation of research over the whole field of education' (Blackwell, 1950). The second Foundation title was *The Allocation of Primary School Leavers to Courses of Secondary Education*, written by A. Watts and P. Slater, which addressed one of the major duties given to LEAs by the Education Act of 1944 (Watts and Slater, 1950). The newly licensed Newnes Educational Publishing Company marketed these first two NFER titles at a cost of one guinea (£1.05) and seven shillings and sixpence, respectively.

Another major change took place as 1949 drew to a close with the announcement that Sir Peter Innes would retire and that Mr Ben Morris would succeed him as the Foundation's second Director. (Another of the short-listed candidates on this occasion had been Dr Jacob Bronowski, who achieved considerable media fame as a broadcaster.)[1] Morris, who took up this post in May 1950 at the age of 39, had lectured in education in the University of Glasgow. He had then attained the rank of Lieutenant-Colonel during his war service as a senior psychologist working with officer selection boards in the War Office. From 1947, he was the Chairman of the Management Committee (i.e. effectively the Chief Executive Officer) at the Tavistock Institute of Human Relations in London. Morris had also served on the National Education Committee of the Fabian Society.

In the 1950–51 financial year, the Foundation showed a deficit of nearly £2,300, and this followed the previous year's deficit of almost £2,700. Up until then the Foundation had operated well within its resources, but the expanded programme of activities now necessitated a substantial increase in income. The Ministry of Education had given a grant of £5,000 for 1950–51 and pledged £6,000 for the next year, but it was made clear that the Minister would expect the Foundation to seek an increase in the level of subscriptions from its own corporate members.

The Foundation's next two publications appeared during 1950–51. One was on the education of children with cerebral palsy by M. I. Dunsdon, which marked the beginning of a long tradition of published research by the Foundation into the education of children with special educational needs (Dunsdon, 1952), and the other was the survey into rewards and punishments in schools, to the genesis of which reference has already been made (Highfield and Pinsent, 1952). This weighty tome, containing all the evidence which had been presented to the researchers on this issue, sold for two guineas.

The research programme at this time included an investigation into the effects of systematic coaching on the performances of children in the grammar school entrance examination, an issue of particular concern at this period, and another study concerned with an evaluation of the effects of films and filmstrips on children, an indication that, even before television had begun to penetrate most homes, the influence the visual media might have on young minds was a matter for debate.

   The Foundation was increasing its contacts too with the wider educational world both at home and overseas. A library was starting to be organised and enquiries to the Foundation were continuing to flow; staff were being invited to address meetings of educational organisations and the Director was reported to have visited a number of university centres and to have been invited to participate in an UNESCO conference in Paris. Relations with the Scottish Council for Research in Education (SCRE) were reported to be particularly close.

Note

[1] Dr Jacob Bronowski was a member of the *Brains Trust* panel and presented a much-praised television documentary series, *The Ascent of Man*. Bronowski's referees for the NFER appointment had included two other renowned individuals, C. P. Snow and Julian Huxley (Clarke, n. d.).

Chapter 3

The Crucial Years
1951–1960

It was at this period, however, that what Yates described as 'The Crucial Years' broke upon the Foundation. The introduction to the 1951–52 Annual Report sounded the alarm bells: 'Preoccupation with budgetary issues, severe financial stringency...[and]... an atmosphere of chronic uncertainty regarding the future are conditions prejudicial to the mental composure required for the reflection and long-term planning so essential in research.' In these parlous circumstances, the new Director, Ben Morris, prepared a pamphlet, *The Case for Doubling*, which was circulated to all the Foundation's members, and took on the task of travelling the country to proclaim the need for an increased income to safeguard the NFER's future. The two principal providers of income, the LEAs and the teachers' associations, were asked to pay a halfpenny (1/2d) per pupil and £12 per thousand of their members, respectively. The country's post-war financial situation was difficult, however, and a number of authorities intimated that they would withdraw from membership in the light of this doubling of subscription. This was a grave matter because the LEAs provided the largest source of income and, as the Annual Report stated, without their support the Foundation 'cannot claim to be truly national...[and]...it has to be emphasised that the organisation's future is almost entirely in their hands'. It was also stressed that, even with the increased rates of subscription, four-fifths of the authorities would pay less than £60 per annum from the rates when the grant allowed by the Ministry of Education for research purposes was taken into account. The result of the increased subscription in 1952 was the loss of 24 LEAs from membership, whereas previously almost all had subscribed.

Sir Fred Clarke, who was arguably the Foundation's principal founder, died in January 1952. A history of the London Institute of Education has described its former Director as 'wise, calm and gently humorous' and as being at his best with small groups of students (Dixon, 1986:29). In a black-bordered obituary tribute in the Foundation's Annual Report, the Executive Committee recorded its deep sorrow at his passing, describing Sir Fred as '...perhaps the leading educational philosopher of his day...an elder statesman in the practical conduct of educational affairs [and] a devoted servant of the cause of educational research'. As well as bringing the influential support of the Institute to set up the NFER, Sir Fred had also acted as an adviser to the National Union of Teachers, which gave vital funds to the Foundation in its early years (Mitchell, 1967). A large bronze plaque to the memory of Sir Fred Clarke, proclaiming him as 'A Founder and Faithful Friend', was later commissioned by the Executive Committee and is now displayed in the reception foyer of the Foundation's headquarters at The Mere.

Portrait of Sir Fred Clarke by Raymond Coxon, 1950, at the Institute of Education

During this period there was a growing involvement with test construction and with the distribution of tests produced in other countries. As well as its own Test Services, a Test Import Agency was formed when agreement was reached with the Australian Council for Educational Research and the Psychological Corporation, USA (then the largest professional organisation in the world devoted to tests services) for the Foundation to act as the sole agent for the importation of their tests for use in this country. Problems had, however, been experienced in relation to the import of such material in respect of both currency exchange and import duties. The writer of an article in the NFER's new journal, *NFER Bulletin*, complained that tests

> *...may be variously classed as 'Stationery', 'Toys' and 'Picture Cards', each category having its own rate of duty and tax ...* [and that] *under present circumstances it has been found that delivery, even at its swiftest, cannot take place under three months from Australia and six months from the USA, and clients should bear this in mind when ordering test material.*
>
> (Morgan, 1953:25)

The first contacts were reported with the Educational Testing Service at Princeton in the USA. Morris was aware that the Foundation's work in this area had to be firmly rooted in the practical requirements of the practitioners when he wrote:

> ...tests which might be of great theoretical interest, but which can only be used by trained workers, or which arouse opposition, have to be kept to a minimum. The practising teacher is very understandably on guard against methods which savour too much of the laboratory, and he tends to be sceptical of the efforts of investigators with no obvious understanding of conditions obtaining in the classroom.
>
> (Morris, 1952:38)

One of the most significant developments in 1953, in addition to the steps taken towards a resolution of the Foundation's financial problems, was the adoption of a *Statement of Policy*. After six years of active existence, in which it had been necessary to concentrate on creating a stable framework, it was thought opportune to produce a policy statement indicating the general direction in which it was intended to develop its work. As Alfred Yates commented: 'It is a testimony to the spirit of the Foundation and to the extent to which it felt able to rely on the continued loyal support of its members that such a document, setting out the guide-lines for a long-term research programme, should have been actively prepared at a time when it was reduced to a precarious hand-to-mouth existence' (Yates, 1971:7–8).

The Statement sought to articulate the policy principles by which the Foundation would operate and to define its responsibilities and relationship with other organisations. In a highly detailed document, the Statement indicated that: 'The Foundation's primary concern was the study and resolution of practical problems arising within the public system of education...' and in a further key passage it was declared that:

> The Foundation will concentrate on problems of educational guidance, in a wide sense of that term. Educational guidance is defined from this standpoint as one way of looking at the teacher's major functions. It means the use of suitable methods of teaching and the provision of adequate opportunities for learning and personal growth. It means relating what is taught and learned, on the one hand, to the needs, powers, interests and experience of children, and, on the other, to the needs, responsibilities, opportunities and values of

adult life. The Foundation's basic programme will, therefore, be designed to assist teachers to discover abilities and aptitudes, to demonstrate the most suitable methods and materials of learning, and to indicate the standards of achievement which can reasonably be expected.

(NFER, 1953:3)

Three broad areas would be covered by the Foundation's research programme: guidance on primary school teaching methods with special reference to standards of attainment in language and number; the allocation and transfer of pupils from primary to secondary schools and guidance in secondary schools, and related problems. Such a detailed statement indicated that the early *ad hoc* collection of research activities was now to be replaced by a coherent planned programme: the infant organisation was now coming of age.

The period 1953–54 saw a more confident note resumed, with the work of the Foundation becoming much better known in this country and abroad, an increase in the scope of its activities and also a marked improvement in its financial position, with a return to a surplus balance over the years 1952 to 1954. By now there were 17 LEAs not in membership, compared to the 24 in the previous year. The objectives indicated in the *Statement of Policy* were being implemented, and efforts to bring about greater coordination of research among the various bodies in the country were also yielding results. A journal entitled *Bulletin*, published twice a year, had been introduced in March 1953 to spread information about the Foundation's work: in its second issue, Alfred Yates had written that 'research workers have begun to abandon their nomadic existence... and are settling down as resident members of those communities with whose problems they are actively concerned' (Yates, 1953:26).

At the sixth Annual Meeting of the Foundation, Sir Godfrey Thomson – a pioneer of educational research and famous for his work on the measurement of human abilities who had held the Chair of Education in the University of Edinburgh and had a long association with the Scottish Council for Research in Education – was elected as a fourth NFER Vice-President. He addressed the Council that year on the tensions inherent in educational research: 'I think that research is best when inspired and carried out by an individual; best when it is a free activity and not carried out under orders; best when it has fundamental problems in view and not the mere solving of practical difficulties. But in this naughty world, as the prayer book has it, these conditions are seldom possible in any form of research, and practically never possible in educational research.' (Thomson, 1953:11). Sir Godfrey, who had given support to the Foundation from its early days, was to occupy this honorary office for but a short period before his death in 1955.

The Association of Education Officers was admitted to membership during 1955, an event which was thought worthy of approving comment: 'There is no doubt that this direct link with the senior executive officers of local education authorities will be a great advantage... [it] is a consequence of the increasing interest chief education officers have been taking in the work of the Foundation.'

Test Services were now offering 36 standardised tests which they had constructed with over half a million copies of tests having been sold since 1950. Douglas Pidgeon succeeded Dr MacFarlane Smith as Officer-in-Charge of Test Services and a future NFER Director, Alfred Yates, who had joined the Foundation in 1951, was appointed Officer-in-Charge of the Research Programme.

A large-scale study, undertaken in collaboration with the Middlesex Education Committee in the Borough of Twickenham, had followed the progress of groups of children on their transfer to secondary schools to ascertain how satisfactory the allocation methods were and how these children subsequently progressed. Kent County Council had also instituted a study into reading, writing and arithmetic. These were tangible signs of the Foundation engaging with the issues that concerned the local education authorities and an indication that the declarations in the *Statement of Policy* – 'Emphasis will be laid throughout on the practical problems facing teachers and administrators and on research into workable methods for the classroom guidance of the individual child' – were being implemented.

An aspect of the Twickenham inquiry was the follow-up visits conducted into the home circumstances of about 100 of the children whose performance had been at variance with the progress that had been forecast. Similar studies of the progress of children after secondary transfer were being conducted in Southport, Swindon and Wallasey. Research conferences involving different parties were organised at the Foundation to consider issues arising from these various studies. As well as the *Bulletin*, copies of 'Research Memoranda' were issued to corporate members to keep them in touch with the research programme.

The Foundation began to extend its programme of research in the field of secondary education in 1954–55 with a study of secondary technical education (Maclure, 2000:58–62), one of the three strands of the tripartite system of schooling provision. Professor William Wall, the Foundation's third Director, related how he had met with a very senior official at the Ministry of Education to discuss the research: this particular civil servant had expressed to him his astonishment on discovering that technical education even existed in secondary schools in this country.

Ben Morris spent two months in the USA in 1955 during which he looked at developments taking place in American educational research and testing. It is believed that a conference which Morris attended at that time in Atlantic City, organised under the auspices of the American Educational Research Association and supported by UNESCO, was the first international conference on educational research to be held. Among its resolutions was a call for greater exchange of information and cooperation in educational research and for the development of common methods of measurement internationally.

At the end of September 1956, Morris resigned after six-and-a-half years as the NFER's Director to take up the post of Professor of Education and Director of the Institute of Education at the University of Bristol. There had been considerable developments during his tenure of office, in respect of both publications and test production. By 1955, 40 standardised objective tests for the use of local education authorities and teachers were available, ten times the number that the Foundation was able to offer in 1950. An increasingly wide programme of research had been launched and the Foundation's second Director had also overseen the sucessful presentation of the case for increased subscriptions and the preparation of the *Statement of Policy*, all of which had contributed to the increased standing of the Foundation among its corporate members and other educational institutions.

According to Yates, not everyone, however, appreciated the contributions that could be made by educational research during that period in which the Foundation was establishing itself. He relates that Sir David Eccles, then the Minister of Education, and President of the Foundation, had given an opening address at the NFER's Annual Council meeting in 1956 during which he had characterised educational research as 'an activity imposed by the long-haired on the long-suffering', a jibe which Yates, who was on the staff at the time, did not think was altogether jocular (Yates, 1971:9). Eccles, in his second term of office in 1961 at the Ministry of Education, later redeemed himself by pledging increased support for research activities and paying a glowing tribute to the Foundation's particularly effective contribution to this work: '…in spite of his dandified image and nickname of "Smarty Boots", Eccles acquired a considerable reputation as a vigorous and imaginative minister' (Aldrich, 2000:119). Eccles fell victim to Harold Macmillan's purge of his Cabinet in July 1962.

Professor William Wall, Director, 1956–1968

The successor to Morris was Professor William Wall, who had been Reader in Education at the University of Birmingham Institute of Education. He then served from 1951 as the Head of Education and Child Development at UNESCO in Paris before his appointment as the Foundation's third Director. During the 1950s, the Foundation went on strengthening its influence both at home and abroad. The growing reputation of the NFER was now reflected in the increasing number of meetings to which the new Director and members of his staff were invited and the number of LEAs which sought advice from the Foundation. In September 1955, the first conference of the Foundation's members was held at the University of London Institute of Education, attracting an attendance of about 200. Regional conferences of members were to follow at Manchester in 1958 and Swansea in 1959. The States of Jersey opted to join the Foundation's membership in 1959. On the domestic front, another of the influential figures in the Foundation's history joined the staff when John Fox, who was to play a major role in the Foundation's future expansion, was appointed Administrative Officer in 1959 to succeed Mr N. A. W. Le Grand, who had overseen the administration for five critical years. The Foundation's financial worries continued, however, and a further doubling of income from the LEAs, and proportionate increases from other corporate members, were proposed from April 1956.

In April 1957, the Council mourned the tragic death of another of its staunch supporters, Dr George Jeffery, who had served the Foundation well in the role of Chairman of the Executive Committee since 1949 (see Aldrich, 2002 for biographical details). Lionel Elvin, his successor as Director of the University of London Institute of Education, also later joined the Foundation's Executive Committee but Elvin did not assume its chairmanship, as had his two immediate predecessors. In a letter dated 6 December 1960, Elvin notes that: 'The Chairman of the Foundation's Executive Committee was always the Director of this Institute until, at the time of the interregnum between the death of my predecessor here and my own appointment, it was necessary to find another Chairman without waiting' (Clarke, n. d.). Jeffery's successor as Chairman was Sir Wilfrid Martineau, a solicitor and prominent Birmingham local politician, who had been President of the Association of Education Committees and the leader of the local authorities' panel on the Burnham Committee.

During this period the Foundation's library collection was reported to have been classified and placed under the supervision of a qualified librarian. A decision was taken to set up an Information Service to collect and classify research information from this country and abroad. Nine European countries met and agreed to set up an abstracting system and to supply these abstracts to each other: a similar agreement was reached with representatives of British universities to cover published work in this country.

In November 1958, the *Educational Research* journal was launched to provide a more substantial and frequently published journal replacing the Foundation's slim-line *Bulletin*, regarded by Yates as having been 'little more than a modest house magazine' (Yates, 1971:10), of which 11 editions had appeared between 1953 and 1958. Soon, print runs of each edition of the recast journal had grown to 4,000 copies. (Included in the first three editions of *Educational Research* that made up Volume One of the Foundation's new journal, were articles on the teaching of reading and arithmetic; the influence of class size; and school type differences in relation to ability and attainment, all of which form issues of continuing debate.) A series of *Occasional Publications* in an inexpensive format for specialised research documents was also begun.

The new Director's strong connections with other countries brought its rewards. The second meeting of European Centres of Educational Research took place at Eltham Palace in south-east London in June 1958 at which representatives from the USA, Israel and UNESCO were also present. It was at this meeting that the decision was taken to start the International Association for the Evaluation of Educational Achievement. The first recorded mention of international comparisons of attainment in the Foundation occurred with a survey of children of ten to 11 years of age in this country and those of the same age in Queensland, Australia. Negotiations were also under way for the use of the Foundation's tests in this age range for experimental purposes by the University of California in Berkeley.

Dr Joyce Morris, a leading reading researcher at the NFER, 1953–1965

An insight into the experiences of the Foundation's staff in these early years is provided by Dr Joyce M. Morris, who had arrived in September 1953 as an enthusiastic young English specialist to take up the post of research officer for what became known as the 'Kent Reading Enquiries'. Her reminiscences reveal how then, as now, a researcher's lot makes more than just cerebral demands. Dr Morris has related how, jolted out of her romantic reveries of how Robert Browning, en route to woo Elizabeth Barrett, may once have passed by the very house occupied by the Foundation's offices in Wimpole Street, she encountered the harsh realities of fieldwork when visiting 60 Kent primary schools for the *Reading in the Primary School* study (Morris, 1959). Colleagues were eager to learn of her colourful tales from 'the hop fields', experiences which had included a two-hour wait in the snow for a country bus and a more blood-warming encounter with an enormous guard dog performing its duty at a one-teacher rural school. The lack of library resources at the NFER, and the absence in those days of photocopiers and word processors, meant that she had to make meticulous records on specially prepared forms and cards while conducting her background literature searches at the University of London's libraries. Staff shortages prompted a request on one occasion that she help parcel up tens of thousands of the Foundation's test papers. 'I remember my fingers bleeding from contact with the tough, wiry string provided for that purpose, and returning the next day armed with thick, gardening gloves to prevent further damage to hands needed for recording research data', she recalled (Morris, 1996:12–15). Despite these practical problems, Dr Morris's work was well received and a ten-year longitudinal investigation finally resulted in *Standards and Progress in Reading* in 1966 (Morris, 1966).[1]

The issues of testing, and the means by which children were allocated to the various types of secondary education, were of profound significance to the Foundation in the 1950s. In December 1952, Watts, Pidgeon and Yates had published their report on *Secondary School Entrance Examinations*, a study of the factors influencing scores in objective tests, particularly coaching, and the allocation of primary school leavers to courses of secondary education. This 'most timely publication' was welcomed by Florence Horsbrugh, then Minister of State for Education and President of the Foundation, in her annual address to the Foundation as 'having served to put in proper perspective many conflicting claims' made over the preparation for secondary school admissions and had enabled the Foundation 'to show exactly where weaknesses occur in present procedures, while dispelling unfounded anxieties regarding the general reliability and validity of modern methods of examining and mental testing... In doing this the Foundation has striven to serve the public interest by making criticisms where these are called for without undermining confidence in the very great efforts being made by the education service...'

Nevertheless, the 11-plus studies at the Foundation during this time were to lead to a growing awareness that tests had limitations as predictors of secondary school success. Pidgeon and Yates' later work, *Admission to Grammar Schools*, published in 1957, concluded that each year at least ten per cent of children were allocated to the 'wrong' school. It was a publication described by one Director of Education as having become, by virtue of its constant use for reference purposes, 'the grubbiest book in his office' (Yates, 1971:10). Stuart Maclure, the educational journalist and historian, has spoken of the 11-plus research as having made the Foundation really newsworthy for the first time. Enormous interest was prompted by the fact that the NFER, which had partly built its reputation on intelligence tests, was now itself exposing flaws in their reliability and integrity. In an interview with Nick Tester, Maclure said 'As a result I have often thought the Foundation's studies during this period contributed greatly to a breakdown of confidence in selection, which was more significant than any expression of confidence in comprehensive education.'

The impact of these studies, carried out in different parts of the country, was such that they helped to change what had been one of the Foundation's main functions. While not an opinion that he particularly shared, Yates quoted a Foundation member who expressed the view that '...the Foundation helped to carry out the 11 plus efficiently and helped to kill it', appreciating that this was how the NFER's contributions to these changes would have been viewed by some observers (Yates, 1977). Nevertheless, selection was not wholly killed off and it continues to operate in a limited number of authorities in England with the NFER still providing tests for this purpose. Chris Whetton, who has headed the Foundation's test development activities since 1982, commented on this issue at a later time when testing returned to the forefront of debate with the introduction of the National Curriculum: 'It was the selective system that was at fault more than the tests – the tests were about as fair, reliable and accurate a means of prediction as you could have had at the time. In seven out of eight cases the prediction was right' (Dean, 1987:13). Belief in intelligence tests, so highly valued at the start of the 1950s, was nevertheless affected to the extent that they came later to be used more as research tools to assess operational rather than innate ability, with the Foundation leading the move away from 'arid psychometrics' to a more observational and flexible approach' (Pyke: 1996:15).

Note

[1] Dr Joyce M. Morris, whose distinguished career, begun at the NFER, led to the award of the OBE for her work on literacy, has written a memoir. This includes mention of how the reading research she undertook at the Foundation was regarded at the time by Sir Cyril Burt, Sir James Pitman (the advocate of the initial teaching alphabet, or i.t.a.) and some of the teachers' unions. She had been forewarned by her NFER colleague, Dr A. F. Watts, that her research might well cause unease amongst those of influence whose ideological and political opinions were challenged by her conclusions (Morris, 2002a; 2002b).

Chapter 4

Pastures New
1961–1970

As the Foundation grew, the problems of accommodation at 79 Wimpole Street became acute, despite the basement of the nearby 7a Welbeck Street having been leased as overflow office premises. An Annual Report for the beginning of the 1960s commented that the Wimpole Street office 'is not constructed to withstand the very heavy deadweight [from] the tens of thousands of tests from the National Survey... it is becoming imperative to seek further and better accommodation.' Professor Wall told how, when he arrived at the office one morning, he had to climb over the plasterwork from a collapsed ceiling which had given up the unequal struggle to hold the weight of test papers above it. The decision was taken to move the Foundation's offices out of the expensive property market of London's West End and a number of potential locations around the country were considered, including Birmingham and Hartlepool. The solution was eventually found when the Borough Education Officer for Slough, Charles Smyth, drew the attention of the Director, Professor William Wall (who was a nearby resident of that area himself) to a property on the southern edge of Slough. The Mere had stood empty after it had been purchased from Mrs Lucy Bentley by a property developer whose plans to build high-rise blocks of flats on its surrounding acres of grounds had been thwarted (see Appendix 1). The 1962–63 Annual Report described the Foundation's future headquarters as '...a close replica of a black-and-white Tudor mansion...in two acres of land near the centre of Slough [whose] surroundings are quiet and dignified, and the immediate grounds are park-like with flower beds, wide lawns and bushes of azalea and rhododendron', premises which would both provide accommodation for 70 staff members and permit further expansion. Sir Edward Britton has recounted that, ironically in the light of subsequent developments, the NFER's Council deliberated hard and long over whether The Mere was a

The Mere, the NFER's headquarters in Slough

property which was too large for the Foundation's needs. Slough was also conveniently close to London and had good rail connections with the capital. Some canny property negotiations then followed. The NFER had both to extricate itself from the 999-year lease granted by the Howard de Walden Estate, which was intent upon benefiting itself from the increased value of 79 Wimpole Street since it had been acquired by the Foundation, and also had to contend with the developers of The Mere, who attempted to retain a part of that estate's land. The local authority had also taken the opportunity to acquire a portion of the Bentleys' former acres but, fortunately, left sufficient surrounding parkland to be enjoyed by future generations of the NFER's staff and visitors.

By the time the move took place in 1964, however, it had already become necessary both to retain the London premises and to plan to build a permanent extension at Slough, a proposal that then became subject to new office development control legislation. The Wimpole Street premises continued to be occupied until 1972, the London office being under the direction of Douglas Pidgeon and, later, Clare Burstall. (There was also a small unit maintained in Cambridge at this period under Dr Robert Thouless.) Temporary office accommodation had to be built on the old tennis court at The Mere to house the 109 staff who were by then employed in the Foundation's bases in Slough and London. As an interim solution, the Foundation acquired additional accommodation in a new block of offices, Erin House, in Slough's High Street, to which the Statistical and Accountancy Services moved in June 1968. An unwelcome inheritance for the new Director, Dr Stephen Wiseman, was the ongoing saga of the Foundation's attempts to extend its accommodation at its Slough headquarters. In the Annual Report for 1968–69, he observed, with barely contained frustration, that 'To recount the detailed story of our efforts [to provide an extra building at Slough] …over the past five years would… provide a fascinating study of decision-making at national and local level [but] it is perhaps best for the raw material to remain buried in our files.'

The manner in which the estate had been carved up at the time of its disposal also caused a complicated land ownership and leasing situation within the boundaries that the Foundation occupied. The plans for The Mere had to be repeatedly revised to meet the expansion in the Foundation's activities and Slough Borough Council eased the difficulties being experienced by granting the Foundation the use of the Bentleys' former garage (currently the NFER's Print Shop), which it then owned. Discussions were also under way with the local authority to ascertain if a new main access could be obtained. A CLASP (Consortium of Local Authorities' Special Programme) constructed building, i.e. one made of modular parts, which offered savings in both time and money, was ordered after the NFER's Director and Secretary had been impressed by a visit they made to the University of York. The architects to that university, Messrs Robert Matthew, Johnson Marshall and Partners, were appointed to build the Foundation's extension in Slough. The main building work on the permanent extension to The Mere was finished by the end of March 1972 and, following its equipping and the restoration of the surrounding area, all staff had moved to Slough by the end of July. The London premises were then put up for auction in September 1972.

The Mere cost the Foundation £30,500 and, while another £64,000 was spent in adapting and expanding its new premises, the sale proceeds of 79 Wimpole Street, yielding £303,000, had more than comfortably covered the costs of the fine new headquarters in which the Foundation could have great pride. The surplus arising from the sale of the central London premises, which had been leased for £9,500 in 1947, enabled the Foundation to set aside a sizeable sum in a capital fund. The loan from the National Union of Teachers to purchase the lease of the NFER's first headquarters had therefore also served to provide, by way of inflated London West End property values, a handsome financial legacy for the Foundation. Professor Wall, the Director at the time of this move, has expressed the highest regard for the skill and devotion demonstrated by John Fox, who headed the Foundation's administration for many years, both for the work he performed over the relocation and for his careful stewardship of the Foundation's finances.

An unexpected inheritance when the Foundation moved to The Mere was the discovery that it had a long-time resident living rough in its grounds. Dick Walton, who was 65 at the time his tale was told, was reported to have occupied a potting shed (he called it his 'tin villa') in amongst the shrubbery for at least a decade before being rehoused by the Slough Council. Dick had once been a gardener's boy when the Bentleys still occupied The Mere. This employment and his long occupancy had enabled him to 'know the topography and history of these grounds like the back of his hand – where the cultivated raspberries may still be found in season [and] the Prospect point [one of a number of elevated mounds that were previously to be found in The Mere's grounds]... which once gave uninterrupted views of [the neighbouring] Herschel Park to ladies and gentlemen taking the evening air'.[1] He recalled all the lodge houses that had once also stood about the estate and the ornate lamps that had illuminated the driveway: less romantically, he described where the watercress beds had been and how, when they fell into disuse, they became infested with water rats. Dick Walton, whose life appeared to have been full of colourful and eccentric episodes, was a living link with a vanished past. To some of The Mere's new occupants, however, he seemed like a Gothick hermit occupying his leafy lair in the shadow of the neo-Tudor mansion house. Even after his resettlement in Council-provided accommodation, Dick secreted the necessary utensils in the grounds of The Mere so that he could return to boil up a billycan of tea in his previous haunts for old time's sake.

The 1960s were a decade which heralded a period of extensive change at the NFER. Not only did the Foundation move to a new headquarters, but it also greatly increased its staffing and the range and number of its research projects and sponsors. The results of this research were to produce a great increase in data and vital developments in the technology which processed that information. It was also a period which witnessed a significant change in attitude towards educational research and the establishment of a number of national advisory and funding councils. The end of that decade also saw the appointment of a new Director at the Foundation and the demise of influential individuals who had played a major role in guiding the NFER since its earliest days.

The deaths of the two men who had had much to do with the establishment of the Foundation in its formative years, the first Director, Sir Peter Innes, and the first administrator, Lea Perkins, were reported at the beginning of this decade. The loss of two other loyal supporters, Sir Frederick Mander, one of the Foundation's three Vice-Presidents, and Sir Wilfrid Martineau, the Chairman of the Executive Committee, was also mourned a few years later in the 1963–64 Annual Report. Mander, a former NUT General Secretary, was a Director of the Newnes Educational Publishing Company, which had, in the NFER's early years, the exclusive rights to publish the Foundation's reports. Martineau, described as being of a 'gentle, friendly presence', had chaired the Executive Committee through some exacting years between 1958 and 1963. In succession to Martineau, Sir Francis Hill was appointed Chairman of the Executive Committee.

A towering figure in the world of educational administration in this country, Sir William Alexander, the Foundation's first Treasurer, resigned in 1966 from the NFER's Finance and General Purposes Sub-Committee and its Executive, on which he had served since 1947. Alexander served as Secretary of the Association of Education Committees for 33 years during which he became '...the public face and authoritative voice of English education' (Newsam, 2002:1). More than one Director of the NFER, however, had had reason to feel ambivalent about the presence of Alexander's dominant personality on the Foundation's governing body.[2] Another of the trio of Vice-Presidents appointed in 1948, Sir Samuel Gurney-Dixon, died in April 1970.

Amongst the announcements in these Annual Reports about the many knighted educationalists who guided the Foundation's progress, there is also to be found a more personal note, with the first officially recorded marriage in July 1961 between NFER colleagues, Sheila Bate, an Assistant Research Officer, and Mr A. Unwin (the listing of staff in the Annual Reports at this time differentiate the sexes by giving initials for the men but recording first names for the women). Other marriages between colleagues who met at the Foundation would inevitably follow over the years and a more contemporary bride on the staff, Lesley Saunders, held her wedding reception at The Mere in 1993.

The start of a new quinquennium in 1962–63 had led the Foundation's Director, Dr Wall, to reflect on the changes that had occurred since the previous five-year period which had begun in 1958. The most important change he identified was in the climate of interest in research from 'What was regarded by many policy-makers and administrators as a marginal, esoteric but relatively harmless activity...[to one]...of fundamental importance to educational reform and the wise expenditure of a thousand or more millions of public money'. During this earlier period, he observed that the Foundation had built up substantial financial reserves which had enabled an integrated research, information and test programme to be developed as a balanced whole. The conduct of increasingly complex and large-scale research programmes in the Foundation had, however, presented problems in terms of the continuity of staffing (recruiting experienced research staff still posed difficulties) and complications in the analysis of data. A significant growth in computer techniques had also profoundly affected the work which researchers were undertaking. The conviction among those at the Foundation that there needed to be the means to collect much more basic data about the work of the education system in this country also became apparent in the national reviews carried out by the Crowther (1959) and Robbins (1963) Committees,[3] both of which were hampered by a lack of the necessary information as they set about their respective investigations.

The source of funds to sustain the work of the NFER has always to be a prime consideration for those who manage the Foundation. As a relatively new discipline, those in education looked enviously at the funds made available at this time to other researchers. In the Foundation's 1960–1961 Annual Report, it was observed that industry spent the equivalent of five per cent of its contribution to the Gross National Product on research with the addition of a further £13 million contributed from public funds by the Treasury. Medical research represented about 0.5 per cent of the cost of the National Health Service. However, empirical research in education did not exceed 0.2 per cent of the total costs of education. And, at this time, there were few foundations or other similar sources in this country on which educational research could call to supplement, to any significant degree, government grants. It was also asserted that a more favourable situation then existed for funding educational research in both the USA and the former USSR than was the case in the UK. These arguments may have influenced the announcement by Sir David Eccles, the Secretary of State for Education, at the thirteenth AGM that the Ministry's grant to the Foundation would be increased from £3,000 to £7,000 for the three years from 1961. Such was the Foundation's pressing need for extra financing that agreement had to be reached in May 1962 with the local authority associations that they would recommend a 75 per cent increase in the subscription paid by LEAs, and with the teachers' unions for a 50 per cent increase in their rates, for the 1963–1968 quinquennium.

The annual accounts indicate the growth in the size of the operation for which the Foundation was responsible, with an eightfold increase in the total budget taking place in the course of a decade. Between 1963–64 and 1965–66 alone, research funds administered by the Foundation rose from £84,000 to £176,000 with the Foundation's total funds, including those of the Test Services and

Agency, having risen to almost £250,000. Even so, the finances of the Foundation were reported to have been under severe strain, especially because of the inflationary costs of that period which had had to be absorbed. To assist with this situation, the DES increased the grant to the Foundation from £7,000 to £20,000 in 1964–65, a figure maintained up to the end of 1966–67, after which it fell to £10,000 per annum.

Two important changes occurred in this period. The first, reported to have caused long and complicated negotiations, involved a change in the constitution of the Foundation in March 1967 from that of an unincorporated association, dependent upon trustees for holding its property, into an incorporated, charitable body. Another very significant change happened in the financial year 1967–68 after which the Foundation would draw its income from local authority pooled funds for research and development work rather than directly from each separate authority as hitherto. The first AGM of the Incorporated Foundation took place in November 1967, at which the Treasurer reported that the local authorities had agreed to support the new pooled subscription rate and accepted the Foundation's triennium estimates for 1968–69 to 1970–71. The Department of Education and Science (DES) had also agreed to continue with its grant of £10,000 per annum for three years.

The burgeoning organisation experienced technical as well as financial difficulties. While it was still lamented that much of the basic information necessary to define topics for research and to set up satisfactory sampling was absent, it was also the case that the volume of data which was coming from educational research was much larger than at any previous time. Time and cost estimates made for projects were also proving too low for the increasingly complex and rich data that was being handled. The Foundation did not have the technical capacity, in terms of all the necessary card punching and sorting machines, as well as a computer, to process all of this incoming data. The NFER had therefore to employ the services of the Department of Statistics at the Agricultural Research Station at Rothampstead in Hertfordshire, as well as using the facilities that were made available by the Central Electricity Generating Board and the University of London Computing Unit. Two commercial companies, United Biscuits and Colgate-Palmolive, also made their Document Readers available for use by the Foundation. Unfavourable comparison was drawn between the modern, technical support available to those conducting similar national surveys financed by the Medical Research Council and the difficulties and costs experienced at this time by the Foundation in processing its statistical work. The Foundation was not alone in being deficient in its technical support, however. The Annual Report for 1961–62, in describing this problem, observed that '...the position will [perhaps] be eased when the Ministry for Education itself possesses a computer.'[4]

In the second half of the 1960s, a reorganisation of the support staff took place, with an augmented Statistical Services taking in members of staff who had previously been attached to particular projects. The Foundation's own Data Processing Unit was established, which meant that there was no longer need to have recourse to outside data processing agencies. Hand punching of cards was still practised but experiments were taking place with a Document Reader which would punch cards mechanically direct from test answer sheets. Advances also took place in the use of computers. Problems had been experienced in getting data processed and programmed by outside computer units and so the Foundation's own Computer Programming Unit was set up at this time. In November 1968, the Foundation installed its own IBM 1130 computer which then enabled the organisation to undertake most of its own data processing and statistical work: it was reported that 'many of the statistical staff are becoming proficient at computer programming'. This made a significant difference: 'All our projects are now feeling the benefit of having a computer on site and the answers to their requests for work often appear on their tables within a day or so of the work being initiated.' A new Programming Section was formed but the Punch Card Section continued to punch 400,000 cards of projects' data as well as taking on the responsibility of punching programme cards for the Computer Section.[5]

Dr Wiseman was quick to appreciate the effects that new technology – as well as a changed approach to the scope of research projects – would make when he wrote that:

With the advent of more efficient and speedy methods of data processing and the acceptance of the computer as an indispensable element of research equipment, we are perhaps in danger of dismissing as unimportant any research project which is not large in scale, wide in range and comprehensive in its coverage of schools and pupils.

By the middle of the 1960s, a large expansion had also taken place in the Foundation's organisation, and changes were afoot which increased its funding and influence. The Annual Report for 1964–65 records that, in the course of that single year, a senior staff of three, the Director, a Deputy Director and a Senior Research Officer, had grown to a complement of eight, with six Senior Research Officers, each one of whom presided over an area of activity as large as was the whole of the Foundation's work in 1958. Compared with the Foundation's own income of £84,000, a further sum of £54,000 now came from sponsors, amongst which were the newly designated Department of Education and Science, the Schools Council, the Home Office and the British Council. Bodies like the Plowden Committee and the Nuffield Foundation were now also providing resources for educational research. The new, well-equipped Data Processing Unit helped staff cope with the more sophisticated statistics being gathered by the Foundation's 12 major research projects. At the same time, local government reorganisation, especially the transformation of the London County Council into the Greater London Council, brought the Foundation into contact with a larger number of education authorities. Such rapid change brought its own problems, however, with the growing complexity of the organisation already leading to questions about communication and the need for better control of research projects within the Foundation. With staff spread between London and Slough, there were also concerns about how the corporate spirit could be engendered among a divided work force.

The Foundation continued to raise its profile both within and outside this country. Staff from overseas research institutes, particularly in America and Australia, were eager to base themselves for a period at the NFER. A team of Venezuelans, who would later set up a national educational research organisation in their own country, were provided with a fortnight's training in research techniques. In 1962, the first of the studies resulting from cooperation with a number of research centres in Europe, America and Asia was published by the UNESCO Institute of Education on the educational achievements of 13-year-olds in 12 countries. Douglas Pidgeon, the Head of the Test Services, spent a year in a university post in the USA and was also appointed joint test editor for the International Evaluation of Attainment Project. The IEA, an international, non-governmental, scientific association which undertakes quantitative research on educational achievement on an international scale, had formerly been directed (until 1962) by Professor Wall. On his return, Pidgeon became, in December 1963, the first to hold the office of Deputy Director in the Foundation.

The Annual Reports at this time listed the involvement and positions of responsibility, in both national and international educational bodies, which were held by the Director, his Deputy and others on the Foundation's staff. For example, amongst a number of positions which he held, Professor Wall was serving as the Chairman of the Education Committee of the National Association of Youth Clubs. Through Professor Wall, there was also an association with the founding of the National Children's Bureau, whose first Director, Dr Mia Kellmer Pringle, had worked with the NFER's Director in his time at Birmingham University. Professor Wall was also co-chairman of the National Child Development Study (1958 Cohort) – which followed the lives of a complete week's births in Britain – whose management was entrusted to what was known at first in 1963 as the National Bureau for Co-operation in Child Care.[6] The Foundation's researchers – most of whom were stated to have had substantial and varied teaching experience themselves – were therefore firmly rooted in the emerging needs of education, amongst whose challenges identified at this time were the education of immigrant children and initiatives to combat the effects of cultural deprivation.

A welcome announcement was given by Sir David Eccles at the Foundation's AGM in October 1961 that his Ministry had formed a Research and Information Branch which, it was hoped, would increase the cooperation between its civil servants and the NFER. The Minister also stated an intention to establish a substantial research fund to assist projects of particular interest to the Ministry, from which the Foundation might well expect to benefit. In this same address, Eccles suggested that, in addition to developing its research work, the Foundation could help by turning out more trained research workers and by increasing its advisory information services to improve communication among research workers and others concerned with education. This was a challenge that the NFER would admirably fulfil.

The Minister's address at this same 1961 AGM was followed by a talk given by Professor E. A. Peel, who, in speaking about priorities in educational research, outlined his views about the relationship between research in the universities and that more appropriately conducted by the NFER. Peel ended his talk with a plea for the establishment of a Council for Educational Research comparable in its financing to that of the Agricultural and Medical Research Councils. The next Annual Report, for 1962–63, made reference to an adjournment debate in the House of Commons on educational research and a proposal put forward by the Parliamentary and Scientific Committee for a Council of Educational Research. In addition to the new Research and Information Branch, a Curriculum Study Group had also been established at this time in the Ministry of Education. The guest of honour at the Foundation's AGM in 1962 was Mr Derek Morrell, leader of this Curriculum Study Group, who outlined the need for a thorough revision of curricula and textbooks, a proposal which was sharply criticised by some of those present, who saw it as a tendency towards a centralisation of authority in education. David Eccles set up the short-lived Curriculum Study Group in 1962 under Derek Morrell, of the Ministry of Education, and Robert Morris, an HMI. 'Opposition from the teachers and local authorities blocked the Ministry's first tentative steps to move in on the curriculum and the CSG was replaced by the Schools Council with Morrell and Morris as two of the joint secretaries' (Maclure, 2000:25).

Professor Wall was tireless in his advocacy of his profession and chaired an organisation called MIER, 'More Interest in Educational Research'. The Foundation's Director was keen to defend educational research against those academics who asserted that it had been 'remote and theoretical without much effect on the practice of the schools'. He traced much of the work that had been done in child development and research in education back to the foundation of the British Child Study Association in 1893 and the studies subsequently carried out by teachers, school inspectors, psychologists and professors of education. As a result of such work, he argued, schools were now

> …more humane places than they were, thanks to our knowledge of individual differences and the dynamics of personality growth; the basic subjects of mathematics and reading are better taught, thanks to solid work on human learning and the causes of failure; we know something about examining and measuring progress, thanks to the psychometrists, and a great deal more than we used, about personal, educational and vocational guidance of adolescents…It seems remarkable that so much has been achieved when probably not more than a few thousand pounds of public money was spent on educational research between 1920 and 1960.
>
> (NFER Annual Report, 1964–65)

The Director also made reference to the involvement of teachers in educational research. It was emphasised that the Foundation had always advocated the involvement of practising teachers in the planning and conduct of research but Professor Wall cautioned that, until colleges of education and universities undertook more training for teachers in research, 'the idea of a profession sensitive to and able to appraise and apply in practice the fresh knowledge which current research will bring' would remain a dream.

The NFER's Director felt it necessary, however, to warn that not all research was as objective as that undertaken at the Foundation, and spoke of educational research becoming

...something of a bandwagon [on which] *individuals and bodies with scanty experience and minimal competence are now turning their attention to matters which they think may provide rapid (and sometimes sensational) returns. Some of these are commercial interests who skilfully conceal their origins or convince a reputable educational organisation that they will finance research without strings. Others are self-appointed pressure groups often with innocent and high sounding titles...Questionnaires are a favourite instrument of such groups, since they appear simple to construct and interesting to fill.*

(NFER Annual Report, 1963–4)

However, the results of most of these questionnaires, he cautioned, had often to be discarded because of their amateurish design and inadequacy of sampling. Wall was also concerned about avoiding duplication of effort and thought it was becoming urgent to have an information service which could gather intelligence on research and provide a databank for research teams to find out whether the information they wished to collect did already exist.

Such was the rapidity of change in this decade that, by the time of the 1965–66 Annual Report, Professor Wall was sounding a note of considerable optimism, even going so far as to observe that the Foundation, which had for many years been urging the necessity for a much higher rate of investment in research, could not

...have foreseen that relatively large sums would be forthcoming so comparatively rapidly. Nor could it have been predicted that genuine interest in, and awareness of, the value of [educational] *research would spread widely in government departments and, indeed, among the general public.*

(NFER Annual Report, 1965–6)

Even the daily press were reported to be carrying an increasing number of well-presented news items about research, although 'it is apparent that the ability to communicate the findings of research clearly and concisely, and in a reasonably objective and balanced way is not common'. The DES themselves had now created a Planning Branch to undertake short-term research studies. Within a couple of years both the Schools Council for Curriculum and Examinations (1964) and the Social Science Research Council (1965) had been established, the latter with an Educational Board under the chairmanship of Lord James. Other organisations had also widened their brief to include educational research, and several other bodies 'which, though their main purpose has been to act as pressure groups, have nevertheless claimed to be undertaking educational research' had been set up. The Schools Council had completed its preparatory year and was said to be 'beginning to find a pattern of activities and finance, which are complementary to those of the NFER'. An Examinations and Tests Research Unit was set up at this time in the NFER, financed by the DES on behalf of the Schools Council, to conduct enquiries on pupil assessment and examinations. The Nuffield Foundation, having entered the field of curriculum development, had also created *ad hoc* units for research and development. A growing number of universities too had set up substantial research projects and a similar expansion was anticipated among the colleges of education. In the midst of such major developments, however, Professor Wall felt it necessary to voice a note of caution:

> *The outstanding problems of national policy and investment however remain those of the proper balance between innovation and research. We have to decide how far we should allow pressure of circumstance and reforming enthusiasm to force us to initiate changes in education unsupported by the slower, less spectacular growth of accurate knowledge about children and their learning, and how far we should allow the claims of innovators to escape objective evaluation.*

Between 1965 and 1967, finance from sponsors increased by 125 per cent and became a substantial part of the Foundation's finance. Some very significant research was initiated at the Foundation at this period. Anthony Crosland, the DES Secretary of State, called together a small working group of interested parties to advise him on the possibility of research into various forms of comprehensiveness in secondary education.[7] The Director wrote that

> *National policy is to move towards an end of the bipartite or tripartite systems, and to abandon allocation as early as eleven. This is a value and political judgement taken on the basis of social and philosophical views and some current educational experience. The Secretary of State made quite*

clear that in this enterprise the function of research is to guide and evaluate experiment, to provide the educational system with a knowledge of the facts and of the ways in which the overall aims can most effectively and economically be obtained.

(NFER Annual Report, 1964–5)

It was recommended that the NFER should be entrusted with an overall executive responsibility for this work, and in 1965 *The Comprehensive Education Project* was initiated. This attempted to assess the extent to which comprehensive schools were achieving their objectives and also surveyed authorities' plans for comprehensive reorganisation. Groups of experts also met for the purpose of trying to define the objectives of comprehensive education. It was a study that was envisaged to last for six or more years and would demand the development of a great variety of psychological and sociological research instruments.

The Director was keenly aware that issues then under investigation by the Foundation, like streaming and comprehensive education, were full of socio-political implications and that 'research in education should be neutral and objective. It should seek to establish the facts, inferences, and alternative explanations, on which choice can be made in the terms that those responsible for policy decide...' and applauded the fact that there was now a 'welcome tendency of policy making bodies to call for evidence as well as opinion'. An encouraging sign was the grant given by the DES to the Foundation to produce a *'Map' of Educational Research*, a project undertaken by Dr Robert Thouless at the Foundation's Cambridge Unit. The report, published in January 1967, covered the whole field of empirical studies in British educational research, highlighting those areas where research would be most profitable or where research efforts were lacking.

Another extensive study at this period was the *Constructive Education Project*, jointly sponsored by the DES and the Home Office, which was designed to look at schools in relation to their respective neighbourhoods and the various influences brought to bear by parents, industry and commerce, and the other local authority services in the community, as well as different pedagogical approaches in the schools. This work was expected to extend over eight years: such lengthy periods of research were not uncommon at this time. In 1964, another major Foundation project, the *Teaching of French in Primary Schools*, was begun, supervised by Clare Burstall. The Foundation was also diversifying its areas of research as illustrated by a one-year survey of medical students undertaken on behalf of the Royal Commission on Medical Education.

The Foundation's Information Service became responsible for a considerable enlargement in the means of disseminating the results of such research. As well as *Educational Research*, and the *Lists of Current and Completed Research*, a new journal, *Technical Education Abstracts*, designed to give information to all those involved in technical education and training, was published from the beginning of 1961 and appeared four times a year. There was also an *Occasional Publications* series.

A further milestone was the appointment of a new Director. Professor William Wall left the Foundation in May 1968 to become Dean of the Institute of Education at the University of London, having occupied the post of NFER Director for 12 years. The Foundation had experienced enormous changes during his time in that office. In 1955–56, the Foundation had a total income of £28,000 and the work was housed in 3,000 square feet of floor space at 79 Wimpole Street. By the time of Professor Wall's departure, the annual budget had risen to £369,000 and it was proving difficult to contain the organisation's activities within 20,000 square feet of office space. From a publications list in 1955–56 which contained only nine research articles and a small bulletin, by 1968–69 the Foundation was producing a major series of research publications, two journals, an occasional publications series, and a paperback series, as well as miscellaneous publications and a newsletter. The outgoing Director was praised for having brought about a change of opinion about the value of research as a key to many educational problems: 'his advocacy of the importance of research, together with his ability to expound the results of the Foundation's research in terms of the day-to-day problems his listeners were facing, had much to do with the change in opinion.'

Dr Stephen Wiseman joined the Foundation as Director in 1968, having previously been the Head of the School of Education at Manchester University since 1957. Wiseman, who had been among the first of the individual members to subscribe when the Foundation was set up, was an influential and respected figure in the field of teacher training and the training of research workers, and well known for his writings on examinations and on the effect of environment on educational attainment.

In his first Annual Report (1967–68), the new Director also provided some illuminating observations on the radical change in opinion and attitude to research in educational circles over the previous few years. He wrote that:

> *Up until the 1950s many teachers, most educationists and nearly all politicians envisaged educational research as a mildly interesting and marginal activity, suitably carried out in the small back rooms of a few universities, supplemented by one or two projects of a more comprehensive nature carried out by the NFER; an activity justifying very little financial support and one with little or no relevance to the formation of educational policy or the development of educational methods. The periodic reports of the Central Advisory Council – that typical British method of providing the bases of educational progress and development – formulated their recommendations by the time-honoured method of canvassing opinion and seeking a consensus.   Recent reports, however, have demonstrated a revolutionary change. Crowther, Robbins and Plowden were not content with merely canvassing opinion – an important part, but only a part, of the decision-making process – they proceeded to seek out facts, and where facts were not available, to commission research to discover them. The consequent increase in the authority of these significant reports has been obvious to all. This clear indication of a new attitude to educational research has been paralleled by an even more important development: the provision of an increasing, although still inadequate amount of money. The formation of the Schools Council, with its acceptance of the view that curriculum development cannot be viable without the support of research; the provision of research grants by the Department of Education and Science; all these testify to the acceptance of educational research as an essential element to support educational development and policy-making…*[The Foundation's] *position of relative independence and political neutrality, and its situation as the only body in England and Wales with a permanent staff of research workers with supporting statistical, computing and administrative services, make it clear that it must occupy a key position in the overall research structure of the country.*

(NFER Annual Report, 1967–8)

The emergence of new advisory and funding bodies at this time also meant that new protocols had to be negotiated. Extensive discussions were held with the Schools Council to clarify the respective roles and relationship between the two bodies. It was agreed that the Schools Council should commission a reasonable amount of work from the NFER each year, particularly in the fields of the technology of examinations and the evaluation of curriculum development where the NFER had unrivalled experience. A solution was also worked out which guaranteed the independence and objectivity of the NFER, both in the conduct of research work and in the publication of results.

The new Director, like his predecessor, lamented the lack of suitably trained research workers which had proved a major hindrance to the expansion of educational research. Dr Wiseman claimed that only the universities of London, Birmingham and Manchester had played a proper part in producing adequately qualified candidates since the Second World War, asserting that their joint output had far exceeded that of all the rest of the universities put together. The others, however, were said to be making valiant efforts to expand such training, which it was anticipated would produce benefits in the coming years. Another promising sign was that the Educational Research Board of the Social Science Research Council (on which, since its inception, Professor William Wall had served) had provided fellowships for the training of educational research workers. It was Wiseman who also observed that 'Educational research is now a highly complex business, demanding the services of many kinds of expert'. He suggested that, while a high proportion of research workers must come from the ranks of the teaching profession itself, this country should follow the American experience of recruiting young graduates, particularly those with degrees in psychology and sociology, to supplement the more traditional pool of educational researchers. This accurately predicted the pattern which the recruitment of educational researchers began to follow in the years to come and which would produce significant developments in the range of different skills that could be deployed for research investigations.

Nearer to home, the new Director also pledged to encourage the Foundation's junior research staff to pursue further appropriate training. In 1967, the Foundation's own Education and Training Scheme was set up to assist members of staff to follow courses in higher and further education. Financial help, study leave, and a loan scheme for textbooks were available to staff. Thirteen members of staff took advantage of the scheme in the first year of operation, entering on courses leading to a variety of qualifications, from A-level to PhD, and a sum of £273 3s 0d was granted that year by the Foundation for staff training.

An important change was instituted in the first year of the new Director's regime when the Foundation took over responsibility for its journal *Educational Research*, by then in its tenth annual volume, which had been published and distributed since 1958 by the Newnes Educational Publishing Company. More emphasis was being placed on a 'straightforward and explicit style and on articles which can readily be understood by teachers'. The need to cater for two principal client groups was clearly identified: 'The Foundation has a dual role to play in producing readable books which will highlight significant findings for teachers and will also disseminate the results of complex studies to other research workers.' In an effort to disseminate information about research, 45,000 copies of *Educational Research News* were distributed by way of the LEAs to schools throughout the country. A designer was commissioned to produce a uniform house style and a 'distinctive colophon' which would immediately identify NFER publications. With press conferences now being organised to launch various NFER publications, sales income was reported to have almost doubled, a trend increased by the adoption of a more realistic pricing structure for the Foundation's publications. The first of the Foundation's pamphlets, *The Challenge of Reading Failure*, based on Dr Joyce Morris's reading survey, had sold 25,000 copies and went into a reprint. The first two of the paperback series, *Planning Small Scale Research* and *The Gifted Child*, had also been extremely well received. Such a growth in the Foundation's output caused Yates to observe that 'An almost nonchalant note [i.e. announcing that "15 or so" publications had appeared] in the Annual Report published in 1970 provides a striking indication of development ...Those old-timers who remembered the days when the publication of a book was the signal for the entire staff to celebrate in the small back room of a neighbouring wine shop must find the phrase "or so" exceptionally piquant' (Yates, 1971:11).

One of the new Director's major frustrations had been to find that the Foundation's own research monies were fully committed for ongoing projects until 1970 and beyond. Dr Wiseman regarded investigations of teachers in the classroom as one of the priority areas for research. A separate Teachers and Teacher Education Division was formed to cover projects in this area – one of which at this time was concerned with the teaching day – looking at the teacher's work both in and out of school. Two of the Foundation's longer-term projects resulted in substantial reports on *French in the Primary School* by Clare Burstall, and Joan Barker Lunn's *Streaming in the Primary School*. Other work in hand included the *Pre-School Project*, for disadvantaged children aged three to five years; a project concerned with the educational progress of immigrant children; and work into vocational guidance, a move made necessary by, amongst other factors, the growth of comprehensive education and the raising of the school-leaving age. A Plowden Follow-Up Project was also undertaken to examine the contribution made by parental attitudes to school achievement. Three major studies were in progress too on monitoring the Certificate of Secondary Education (CSE); attitudes to science; and the Item Bank project, which aimed to produce a library of high-quality examination questions or items which could be used by teachers and examination boards. (Item banks are sets of categorised, trialled and calibrated questions of known difficulty and performance from which selections can be made in order to compile a test of customised content and established difficulty.)

The findings of another project and accompanying criticism at this time were much less palatable, however. Cane and Schroeder's *The Teacher and Educational Research* had surveyed what teachers felt would be of most benefit to them. Its findings caused the Foundation's management distinct unease: only 39 per cent of the teachers surveyed were familiar with at least one piece of work carried out by the NFER and other unflattering comments were reported about their perception of the organisation, and educational research in general. An article published in an educational journal at this time exemplified the criticism to which the Foundation has sometimes been subject and which serves to emphasise the prime need to ensure that its research is always relevant, readable and timely. Michael Pollard, in one of a series of articles entitled 'Sacred Cows', lambasted the NFER for what he perceived were its failures, claiming that 'The inability to tell it like it is is the NFER's greatest problem' (Pollard, 1971:158–9).

One of Pollard's suggested solutions to the Foundation's problems was 'to hire a couple of journalists thick-skinned enough to fight for readability, and to set them to work on the researchers' material'. He praised the research of Joan Barker Lunn on streaming and Joyce Morris on reading, but pointedly indicated that these particular NFER reports had received the attentions of the daily press and so had been rendered by journalists into what he felt was more easily digestible information for both teachers and the wider public audience. 'Teachers need, of course, to know more about matters of vital professional concern than can be contained in 400-word stories in popular papers – but unless research reports can be rendered down into readable form they are unlikely to do so.' Pollard also went on to question the NFER's stance whereby on the one hand its own research advocated non-streaming while on the other it produced tests which were used as the instrument of streaming in hundreds of schools. Should the NFER 'for the good of its soul...engage in a commercial activity of this type', he asked, highlighting a dilemma for the Foundation where the findings of some of its research and the NFER's profitable testing activities might be viewed in some quarters as being in conflict.

Another cold blast of criticism came from an even closer quarter at the Members' Conference in December 1970. Edward Britton, General Secretary of the NUT and the retiring Vice-Chairman of the Foundation, spoke on 'Educational Research: a teacher's view', indicating plainly in his address that he also felt some doubt about certain trends in educational research methods. This teachers' union leader was then followed by Mrs Margaret Thatcher, the Secretary of State for Education and Science and the President of the Foundation from July that year ('the press table increased noticeably, and the delegates filled the room' reported an NFER Research Information Newsletter at the time of her conference appearance [NFER, 1970]). Pollard – no doubt with some journalistic hyperbole – reported the occasion as follows:

> ...if Mr. Britton was merely unflattering, the speech that followed from Mrs Margaret Thatcher was positively sinister. The traditional role of the DES in relation to educational research, the Secretary of State said, had been that of passive supporter. But the limitation of funds necessitated a move away from 'a basis of patronage to a basis of commission'. In other words, the DES, in exchange for the £120,000 or so which it was paying each year to the NFER, was going to expect the right to call the tune.
>
> (Pollard, 1971:159)

This future Prime Minister was already articulating challenging requirements to publicly funded bodies, an approach that she would apply in much greater measure when she later led the country.[8] The Foundation was finding itself challenged anew to meet the particular needs of its clientele, be they in the classroom or the Cabinet, and to adapt to the more stringent funding conditions that would be applied in the conduct of its work.

That mainstay of the Foundation's commercial success, its Test Services and Test Agency, experienced significant growth and by 1962–63 some 2.5 million copies of the Foundation's own tests were being sold, providing a turnover of

£32,000. Each year a new series of 'closed' tests for allocation at 11-plus was produced, consisting of two Verbal Tests and at least one English and one Arithmetic Test. At this time, 12 series of 11-plus allocation tests and four series of advanced 13-plus transfer tests were available to education authorities. 'Open' tests, designed for classroom use to assess progress and individual needs, were also available to teachers. Tests for use in the Foundation's research projects were also constructed. Ginn & Co. Ltd. took over the publication of the 'open' and 'closed' tests from Newnes when the latter ceased to be the Foundation's publishers. The NFER continued to act as a Test Agency for the supply to schools and local authorities of educational and psychological tests produced by other bodies. The Test Agency also transferred to Slough in 1964 and underwent a major reorganisation to improve its service to enquirers.

As interest grew in the use of tests and other instruments as part of a continuous programme of educational guidance rather than merely for 11-plus selection and similar purposes, the advisory function of the Test Services became increasingly important and many enquiries were received from a wide range of interested parties about testing. In 1968, the Test Services were re-designated the Guidance and Assessment Service in order to reflect its expanding activities. The Test Agency, too, had experienced a rapidly increasing appreciation by personnel and training officers of the merits of standardised tests for the recruitment and promotion of staff in commerce, industry and government departments, as well as the use of these tests by a wide range of education professionals. By now, 70 per cent of the tests being sold by the Agency were imported from overseas, although arrangements were made to print some of these in the UK under licence from the overseas publishers. After 1 April 1970, a significant development occurred when the Test Agency was transformed into a subsidiary company, called the NFER Publishing Company, and moved to its own premises at Jennings Buildings, in Thames Avenue, Windsor, where there was adequate accommodation to cope with its rapidly expanding turnover. The surplus from this trading company, which was firmly in the control of the Foundation's Board of Management, was to be ploughed back into the Foundation's funds. A new Publications Division, whose finances were also to be treated separately to enable a constant feedback on performance and financial viability, was also moved to these Windsor premises.

Notes

[1]   'A Nest in the Woods', an unattributed article in the NFER Newsletter, November 1972, p.8, which reproduced information about Dick Walton that had appeared in the *Slough, Windsor and Eton Express* local newspaper, 30 June 1972.

[2]   'William Picken Alexander…was a Scot, a mathematician, a qualified teacher who had done research on psychology and psychometrics at Glasgow …[He was] a strong personality who tended to get his way in argument – a cleft appeared in his chin when he became fully engaged and his piercing eyes had an intimidating effect on those who sought to resist him. Though his title was that of secretary of the AEC, Alexander dominated his executive committee by sheer ability and force of character, leading them through his agenda to make his policy, their policy. He was equally forceful in his dealings with the Ministry and was able to bring influence to bear on policy at the formative (assistant secretary) stage before conclusive decisions had been taken…The NUT had a love-hate relationship with Alexander. They knew he was the bosses' man but also knew he was on their side much of the time' (Maclure, 2000:3–4).

[3]   These Reports dealt with, respectively, education between 16 and 18, recommending the raising of the school leaving age to 16; and the pattern of higher education, with recommendations which led to a significant growth in the number of universities and university places.

[4]   Barnett (2001:366) notes that '…even by 1960 only 250 computers of all types had so far been installed in the United Kingdom, compared with over 1,000 in Europe and 3,800 in America [1959 figure].'

[5]   The electro-mechanical punched card machine was developed in 1889 for sorting and tabulating complex data when its inventor won the competition to process the 1890 American national census. In 1924, the manufacturing company for this machinery became part of International Business Machines (IBM) (Barnett, 2001:356–357).

[6]   See articles by Cooper J. 'The origins of the National Children's Bureau' and Davie, R. 'The impact of the National Child Development Study'(Pugh, 1993).

[7]   Kogan (1978:22) writes that 'changes in local politics followed the 1964 General Election and return of the Labour Government. The bipartisan gradualism on the issue of secondary education was broken by Anthony Crosland's circular 10/65 which requested all local authorities to make their schools comprehensive. Wholesale reorganisation, and local and patchy resistance to it, became the centre of contention in local government.'

[8]   See also Taylor (1973:20), quoting the DES Press Notice, 1 December 1970, which states that the Department's research policy '…meant the active initiation of work by the Department on problems of its own choosing, within a procedure and timetable which were relevant to its needs. Above all it meant focusing much more on issues which offered a real possibility of yielding useable conclusions.'

Chapter 5

Silver Celebrations
1971–1975

In 1971, the Foundation celebrated its 25th anniversary as an independent research institute. The President of the Foundation, Mrs Margaret Thatcher MP, addressed the AGM and a special exhibition was held at that year's conference in Grosvenor House, London. Alfred Yates, described at the time as 'an old friend and past member of staff', produced his personal account of the Foundation's early years which it was hoped would 'appeal alike to those newly acquainted with the Foundation's endeavours and to those many old friends who have indeed helped to shape the very history that has now been recorded'. It has been a work much appreciated by the present author of this Golden Jubilee history of the NFER.

Alfred Yates,
Director,
1972–1983

The 1971–72 Annual Report compared the Foundation's situation in 1946, when the total staff was fewer than six and the work was confined to a handful of relatively small-scale research studies, to that of 1971. By the year of its Silver Jubilee, the staff list contained 158 names and the NFER was conducting an extensive research programme, as well as offering a wide variety of other services to its members and the educational world in general. In 1946, the total income from all sources amounted to £9,000. Twenty-five years later the figure exceeded £424,000.

At this time of celebration for the Foundation, a shadow was cast when Dr Stephen Wiseman, who had suffered increasing ill health since his appointment as Director, died in July 1971. His loss, after just three years in office, was keenly felt by those he had led. The tribute in the Annual Report spoke of his 'utter devotion to the pursuit of truth… a warm heart that sought to encourage, to help, and to befriend… unrivalled scholarship… wisdom and tact'.

Following a short interregnum, Alfred Yates was appointed the Foundation's fifth Director. After war service, Yates had lectured at the Queen's University, Belfast, before spending eight years as a Senior Research Officer with the NFER during its formative stage between 1951–59. He then became Senior Tutor in the Department of Educational Studies at Oxford University, during which time he also acted as a consultant to the Foundation's Board. Yates was impressed by the calibre of staff, both senior and more junior, which he found upon returning to lead the Foundation. The supply of suitably trained staff had also improved, due in some measure to Dr Wiseman's Education and Training Scheme. Among a number of NFER researchers at this period who proceeded to carve out successful and influential careers were Bruce Choppin, Caroline Gipps and Desmond Nuttall.

The late Bruce Choppin was recognised as a leading world expert on item banking and longitudinal testing. After periods in universities abroad, he became a Principal Research Officer and, later, Assistant Head of Research at the NFER until 1981. One of his prime responsibilities was the Assessment of Performance Unit. He was seconded abroad to the International Association for the Evaluation of Achievement for a period and served as Chairman of its International Project Council on Item Banking. Bruce Choppin served as the Treasurer of the British Educational Research Association and was its President for 1980–1981 (see also page 81).

The late Professor Desmond Nuttall began his distinguished career as a researcher in 1967 at the NFER where he became a Principal Research Officer and the Head of the Examinations and Tests Research Unit from 1971–1973 (Murphy and Broadfoot, 1995).

Another change in the Foundation's senior management occurred in 1972 when Dr Douglas Pidgeon, who had been on the staff since 1950 and was Acting Director during the interregnum, took up a new post as Director of the i.t.a. Foundation (the NFER had conducted research into the initial teaching alphabet, on which it published a report in 1966). The first to hold the post of Deputy Director at the NFER, Pidgeon was warmly praised for the outstanding contribution he had made during a career which had included the highly influential studies, with Yates, on the allocation of primary school children to courses of secondary education as well as his responsibility for the Foundation's Test Services. Pidgeon was succeeded as Deputy Director by Clare Burstall, whose skills as both a researcher and manager were highly regarded by the new Director.

Stephen Wiseman had diagnosed soon after his arrival that the NFER's rapid expansion in the 1960s had inevitably exposed certain deficiencies in the organisation and he undertook remedial measures, still incomplete at the time of his death, which Yates then sought to consolidate. The new Director reviewed the internal structure of the Foundation in order to ensure that its resources, both financial and staff, were deployed with the maximum degree of efficiency. He also aimed to secure the fullest possible participation by members of staff at all levels in the conduct of the Foundation's affairs.

On taking office, Yates declared that it was his intention to visit the LEAs and contact teachers, not only to publicise the Foundation but 'to gain information about what kinds of research are regarded as relevant…[as]…the justification for educational research must rest on the contribution that it can make to the improvement of educational practice'. Another area in which he hoped to take a personal interest was the dissemination of the results of research: 'No matter how relevant to our members' interests a particular investigation might be nor how successfully it is carried out, it will make little impact if its findings and, particularly, their implications are not adequately communicated', he declared.

Sir Edward Britton pictured with the NFER Chairman, Mrs Nicole Harrison on his retirement from the Board in 2002

Other significant changes took place within the Foundation and its Board around the time of the change in the directorship. Sir Cyril Burt, associated with the Foundation from its earliest days, and the last of the three Vice-Presidents who were appointed in 1948, died in October 1971. Sir Edward Britton, the former General Secretary of the National Union of Teachers, who was knighted in 1975, retired as Vice-Chairman of the Foundation and Chairman of the Finance and General Purposes Sub-Committee. His outstanding service to the Foundation was continued by his

presence on the NFER's Board until he retired in 2002, after a period of devoted service over nearly half a century which is unlikely to be surpassed. He continues his long association with the Foundation as a Vice-President. Another sundering of the previously close links with the University of London Institute of Education occurred when its Director, Lionel Elvin, retired from the Board in 1972. At this time, two previous Directors of the Foundation, Professors Ben Morris and William Wall, both sat on the Foundation's Board, representing the English Universities.

Within the Foundation itself, a number of reorganisations took place. The Statistical Services underwent extensive changes. Jim Davies succeeded A. E. Sanderson as Head of the Information Division, which now encompassed the Press Office and Exhibitions Section. A new Head Librarian, Janet May, was appointed: the previous occupant of that post, Tony Gwilliam, became Information Officer within the Information Services. A reorganisation of the library book stock took place too and the estate of the late Dr Wiseman bequeathed a collection of his books to the Foundation.

A special press conference was held at the House of Commons in April 1972 at which the new Director was introduced to the educational press and an exhibition on the work of the NFER was opened by its President, the Rt. Hon. Mrs Thatcher, the Secretary of State for Education and Science. A concerted effort was now made to keep the press informed about the Foundation and its activities. A Press Officer, Miss Toni Griffiths, was appointed and she built up a press list of over 450 names, including specialist correspondents and contacts on local, as well as national, newspapers. Press conferences were organised for all major NFER reports and press releases written for all other material produced by the Foundation. A press cuttings and television monitoring service was also introduced. A common house style had been developed and the format of *Educational Research News* – now published three times each year instead of quarterly – was reported to have become 'vastly more pleasing since the arrival of our highly skilled and diligent Press Officer' with 96,000 copies now being circulated. The scope and quality of the Foundation's exhibitions had also increased following the appointment of a specialist Exhibitions Officer, Tim Wright. The Foundation exhibited at 29 different locations during 1971–72, venues that included the Palace of Westminster, the British Council and the assembly of the World Confederation of Organisations of the Teaching Profession.

Yates was well aware that the production of readable accounts of research called for a combination of research expertise and a flair for writing in readily assimilable form. He resolved that the Foundation's publications, while maintaining the same high standards, should attempt 'to simplify the language used and esoteric statistical arguments [should be] avoided in reports and other publications intended for teachers and other educationists'. *Educational Research* had originally been conceived as 'A review for teachers and all concerned with progress in education', but it was felt that it had not succeeded to any real extent in reaching its main audience.

Another innovation was the compilation of critical reviews of significant research projects whilst they were still in progress. Realising that sometimes decisions could not await the period of years it took some projects to complete, it was decided to produce quick and authoritative resumés of relevant research findings together with an interpretation of their apparent implications for the issue under review. The first three such critical reviews looked at compensatory education at the pre-school level; patterns of education in the 16–19 age group; and teaching strategies for dealing with slow-learning pupils. Another change of policy was made to improve dissemination of the Foundation's research findings, *viz.* instead of producing shorter, less technical versions of major reports, as had been the pattern but whose pricing had made them unattractive, such reports were henceforth to be summarised and would appear in the Foundation's journal *Educational Research*. Offprints of such articles would also be available at a low cost.

The London offices at 79 Wimpole Street were, at long last, vacated and finally disposed of by auction in September 1972. This brought to an end the London chapter of the Foundation's history and consolidated its activities largely on the one site at The Mere. This freehold property now owned by the Foundation was estimated by the Board of Management to be worth not less than £185,000. The newly extended headquarters was still unable to house all staff, however, and Erin House in Slough High Street had to be retained to provide a home for the Foundation's computer and related activities, and the Guidance and Assessment Service. The permanent extension to The Mere, brought into full use in the late summer of 1972, housed most of the Foundation's research activities in the main block while a link block provided a Common Room (which also became the staff canteen) and Lecture Room.

The 1972–73 Annual Report recorded that a start had been made on a round of visits to the regional associations of the Society of Education Officers. Conferences and workshops had also been organised with a wide spectrum of interested parties, including teachers, inspectors, HMIs, representatives of the polytechnics and researchers. An invitation to teachers to write to the Foundation if they had proposals for research projects that they would like to see carried out had resulted in a response that was 'most heartening – and almost overwhelming'. Another way in which the Foundation sought to improve the service offered to its members was by acquiring a sophisticated travelling exhibition which displayed a range of literature and was transported in its own van. Thirty-three different venues were visited up and down the country that year. After the Foundation's first Press Officer left, her role was taken on for a short period by a publicity firm. A briefing campaign for leading educational correspondents and feature writers was started and links were strengthened with the BBC's Further Education department and with the Central Office of Information, which recorded a film on the Foundation's work in the field of language disorder.

By 1970–71 the research programme consisted of 18 different projects with a total annual budget of £295,000. The research projects had been grouped in a new framework of Research Services in which each project retained its autonomy but was regularly monitored by the Directorate and the new Head of the Research Services, Dr K. B. Start. A general tightening up of accountability was introduced with planning procedures implemented and the production of running costs every two months for project leaders. Review meetings were also held every three months for all research projects and at regular intervals for the other services.

A number of significant NFER publications appeared at this time. *The Trend of Reading Standards* by K. B. Start and B. K. Wells had attracted considerable attention and it was stated at the time that 'there is little doubt that the Secretary of State's decision to set up a committee of inquiry under the chairmanship of Sir Alan Bullock was to some extent influenced by the results that this survey yielded'. (The Bullock Committee, whose report appeared in 1975, considered all aspects of the use of English in schools, including reading, writing and speech.) *The Reading Standards of Children in Wales* by T.R. Horton was also produced as a comparison to the similar study of English children. Considerable interest had been aroused by the final report of the comprehensive education project: *A Critical Appraisal of Comprehensive Education* by J. M. Ross, *et al.* At the same period, H. E. R. Townsend and E. M. Brittan's *Organization in Multiracial Schools* was praised for the wealth of factual information and the clarity with which it identified problems in this area. Further important work into multicultural education at the Foundation followed by the same two researchers. The fledgling Open University selected one of the Foundation's publications, *Economic Aspects of Education* by M. Woodhall, as a set book. Of especial interest to the research community was A. V. Ward's *Resources for Educational Research and Development*, described as 'the first objective study in this field', which provided a detailed analysis of current expenditure in this area of research.

A very important development was the commission from the DES and the Social Science Research Council at this time for the NFER to establish a comprehensive register of current educational research and development to assist in reducing the duplication of effort and in searching for a new work in any branch of education. A meeting was arranged under the chairmanship of Professor John Nisbet which had a very broad representation of those bodies responsible for research into education, including the DES, research organisations, teachers' unions, universities and national library bodies. It was also agreed that this work should be prepared in a manner which made it readily transmittable to other European countries. *The Register of Educational Research* began in September 1973 and employed the EUDISED (the European Documentation and Information System in Education) thesaurus, which enabled UK research data to be correlated with other data from European countries. This material would later be made available in English, French and German.

By 1972–73, administrative responsibility for the conduct of 22 projects was shared by Principal Research Officers under the Deputy Director, with quarterly review meetings held for each project. A statistician was attached to each project to give expert advice throughout its time. Research sponsored by the Schools Council was taking place into 16-plus examinations, which were now being taken by over half the 16-year-olds in the country. Another study, with the same sponsor, was taking place into the validity and reliability of GCE O-level examinations. Particular emphasis was placed on investigating the effects of allowing candidates a choice of questions and this research also considered the matter of comparability between different subjects. These projects resulted in *British Examinations: Techniques of Analysis* by D. L. Nuttall and A. S. Willmott.

Another strategic development occurred when the Foundation's Book Division was formally transferred in October 1972 to the NFER Publishing Company, which then employed 28 members of staff. Placing the NFER's publishing activities under a commercial company helped them to adapt to the stricter disciplines of trading in a more commercial environment. There had also been a change by now in the book trade's attitude to the Foundation's publications. Whereas previously little interest had been shown in research reports, the successful production and publication of an increasing range of titles by the NFER had led to regular trading with hundreds of educational booksellers at home and overseas. The company soon became recognised as a major outlet for publications in the fields of educational research and development: NFER titles were displayed at major, world-wide exhibitions including the British Council stand at the Frankfurt Fair and at the Tokyo Book Centre, where one exhibition stand was devoted solely to the Foundation's publications. Overseas distributors in Australia, New Zealand and the USA had been appointed, which had widened the potential market for NFER publications. The NFER Publishing Company was also licensed to distribute in the UK research publications from the Educational Research Councils of Australia and New Zealand. A further indication of international interest was the negotiation of translation rights for a Japanese edition of Modgil's *Piagetian Research*: *A Handbook of Recent Studies*. The company's emergence as a recognised publisher was signified by its acceptance into membership of the Publishers Association and its Educational Publishers Council.

Colour printing was now introduced by the company and publications were also produced on behalf of outside institutions, such as the Foundation's begetter, the University of London Institute of Education, and the National Children's Bureau. A number of titles for the latter organisation greatly extended the range of NFER publishing in the area of the social sciences and special educational needs. The Publishing Company's further successes included being invited to publish reports by the Scottish Education Department, the Social Science Research Council and the British Council. Nine NFER books were reprinted to meet demand, two of them being 12-year-old titles. The NFER Publishing Company also became responsible for the publication and distribution of the Foundation's journal, *Educational Research*, and the *Journal of Moral Education*.

The Test Division, which was also now part of the NFER Publishing Company, took over the tests originated and formerly published by the National

Institute of Industrial Psychology, a move which added at a stroke some 3,000 names to its customer list. A Tests and Publications Department, and a Sales Department, were later created. As well as undertaking lecturing and training courses, the Tests Department's work also involved anglicising imported tests, often American in origin, to make them more suitable for use in the UK.

Before its takeover of the Book Division, the Publishing Company contributed a sum of £22,600 in 1971–72 to the Foundation from its profits. By 1975–76, its income had risen to £493,421, with £60,688 paid to the Foundation, and a special thanks was expressed to John Fox, who then held the title of Deputy Chief Executive of the NFER Publishing Company and Secretary to the Foundation.

The senior research team of the Foundation was considerably strengthened by three appointments at Principal Research Officer level during 1973–74. These were June Derrick, who came from York University; Philip Clift, who joined from the Schools Council; and Malcolm Parlett, who had latterly been at the Massachusetts Institute of Technology. One of the 12 research projects completed during this year was accompanied by the publication of *Primary French in the Balance*, by the then Deputy Director, Dr Clare Burstall, and the members of her project team. It was described in an Annual Report as 'the most thorough-going evaluation to which any educational innovation has so far been submitted', having monitored the teaching of French in a number of selected primary schools since it was introduced in 1964. It also declared that: 'The rationale of this project is that before major reforms are introduced into the curricula of our schools, clear evidence should be sought concerning their implications and effects. Many of those who advocate such an approach have identified this study as a model of its kind.'

The Department of Health and Social Security funded a three-year project, from October 1973, designed to compare the standards of some 40 centres carrying out Health Visitor training in the United Kingdom, an early example of what would become the Foundation's long involvement in health-related research projects. The NFER financed the Pre-School Project, action research into the long- and short-term effects of compensatory programmes for three- and four-year-olds, a study which was conducted on the Foundation's doorstep in Slough's nursery schools. Among the range of enquiries reported as having been received at this time by the Information Division were those relating to pre-school education, truancy and disruptive pupils, and disadvantaged and handicapped pupils.

Several other new research ventures were undertaken which furthered the aim to engage with issues that mattered to the Foundation's membership. The first of a number of investigations into aspects of primary school organisation was started in April 1974 looking at the classroom strategies used by teachers. A series of studies of the educational provision for children with different kinds of handicap was planned, the first of which, started in September 1974, was concerned with children who were blind or partially-sighted. The Director claimed that the Foundation's research activities demonstrated that 'no major stage or aspect of the educational system is being wholly neglected' and that the Foundation had 'adopted an eclectic approach to the available range of research methodologies, avoiding whole hearted commitment to any one of the factional interests that compete against each other in this territory'.

The Guidance and Assessment Service also maintained a close liaison with the LEAs and teachers, pioneering the development of new tests and techniques of assessment in responding to demand. The Unit was led by Dr Ray Sumner, who came to be known, understandably, as 'the GAS man' in his extensive peregrinations around the country on behalf of the NFER. Dr Sumner was involved with the emergence of both the EMIE service and the Northern Office, and with surveys that later led to large-scale evaluations conducted by the NFER (Sumner, 1996:24–6). He also organised a successful first meeting, at Cumberland Lodge in Windsor Great Park, of a working party for senior researchers who were engaged on comparable projects in the various member countries of the Council of Europe Committee for Educational Research.

An important domestic development was the decision by the Foundation's staff to form the NFER Social Club in the autumn of 1972. This staff-run venture took on the responsibility for providing coffee and tea during the morning and afternoon breaks, as well as lunch-time snacks: it also held a licence for the sale of alcoholic refreshments. Soon it was able to cater for buffet luncheons, including hot meals, for up to 50 of the 120 or so staff then employed. In January 1974, the NFER Social Club formed an Entertainments Sub-Committee and a revue, a play and a chess tournament were soon organised. The Social Club played an important role in the years that followed by helping to create a congenial work climate for the NFER's expanding band of employees. Outings, sports events, barbecues, barn dances and Christmas pantomimes became an established part of the Foundation's programme of social activities and charitable donations were frequently made from the profits of such events organised by the NFER Social Club. It would not be until 1988 that the Foundation itself took over the management of the staff canteen from the NFER Social Club.

The Foundation's Education and Training Scheme continued to provide support: in 1972–1973, for instance, approximately 27 members of staff received grants of various kinds. These ranged from financial grants (around £600 was paid out in the 1972 academic year) to awards of computer time, paid study leave and day release. Staff assisted by the scheme were reading for PhD, MPhil, MSc and BA degrees and taking courses in librarianship, management studies, statistics, secretarial studies, and a Diploma in Further Education.

Sir Alan Lubbock, a prominent member of the County Councils Association, who had been Chairman of the Board of Management since July 1967, resigned in May 1973 and was elected a Vice-President in July of that year. He was succeeded as Chairman by A. W. S. Hutchings, who was described as 'having set a record of service to the Foundation that is likely to stand unchallenged for a long time'. Hutchings' name had appeared in the first Annual Report in 1947 as a member of the Executive Committee and, from 1970, he had served as Vice-Chairman of the Board and Chairman of the Finance and General Purposes Sub-Committee. Another long-serving member of the Board, and of the Finance and General Purposes Sub-Committee, Mr Charles Smyth OBE, a next-door neighbour in his capacity as Borough Education Officer for Slough, also resigned. He was thanked for having been an 'unfailing source of help and co-operation' whose service to the NFER was recognised by his being made 'an Honorary Individual Member and – the final accolade – the staff have granted him membership of their Social Club'. As earlier described, Smyth had been instrumental in the Foundation's relocation to Slough by alerting a former Director that The Mere was on the property market.

A Conservative politician whose future role as the first woman British Prime Minister was to have profound implications for the educational community, Margaret Thatcher, continued as the NFER's President until May 1974. She was thanked for having taken a 'close personal interest in [the Foundation's] activities and found time to attend our Conferences and exhibitions on a number of occasions' during her four-year period of office. She was succeeded as the

Foundation's President from June 1974 by the Labour Party's Reg Prentice MP, who was in his turn thanked for maintaining 'the as yet unbroken tradition that this role is assumed by the Secretary of State'. Mrs Shirley Williams, another (then) Labour politician who later gained a high national profile, became NFER President from November 1976 in succession to her Party colleague, Frederick Mulley.

The Annual Reports for the early 1970s had recorded a healthy financial position with increased income from the LEAs and the Foundation's book and test sales. The Publishing Company's turnover continued to increase with a large slice of its net profits covenanted to the Foundation providing a useful additional income for research and other NFER services. The Data Processing and Computer Unit within Statistical Services was also increasing the NFER's profitability by selling its services to organisations outside the Foundation, earning £10,000 in 1971–72 from its external clients. The Foundation's total income rose from £425,000 in 1970–71 to £503,000 in 1971–72, with the local authority subscriptions through pooling having increased by £10,000. The Board of Management had also been particularly anxious to ensure that the windfall from the sale of the Wimpole Street offices should be put to the best long-term use through the creation of a capital fund to finance new research.

By 1973–74, however, forces outside the Foundation's control were having their impact and Yates wrote of the Foundation having to operate under 'a gathering gloom of an economic crisis…[with]…fuel shortages and the three-day working week'. The oil crisis and the shortened working week had a peculiar ramification for the NFER's Test Division when, as a consequence of the adverse affects on the plastics industry, it proved difficult to acquire several thousand knitting needles needed for one of their psychological tests.

An explicit warning was sounded the next year about the NFER's finances: 'The swing from the surplus in 1973/74 to the deficit in the year under review must be regarded as a clear indication that the Foundation will have to increase income or curtail activities. With inflation continuing at a high rate into 1975/76, the financial position will require most careful supervision with continuing efforts to secure economies.' National salary awards had contributed significantly to the rise in staff costs which stood at £406,000 in 1974–75, for an average of 130 employees, as compared with expenditure in this same category at £328,000 in 1973–74. There was now a stated intention to reduce the effects of steadily increasing costs: 'To this end we have introduced a number of major economies. We have forgone the luxury of our own computer and have established links with the University of London Computing Centre.' Every item was submitted to close scrutiny and, as a consequence, '…we can lay claim to a creditable collection of candle-ends'. (The entitlement of the NFER's Principal Research Officers to claim for First Class rail travel was a perk that disappeared.) Staffing costs were suppressed and posts downgraded as they became vacant, or were not filled within the administrative, information and statistical services. In addition to the extra income generated by making the Foundation's data processing and statistical analysis facilities available, another way of supplementing income was found by staff acting as paid consultants on research design, evaluation and test construction on behalf of organisations both in this country and overseas. During 1975–76 this source of income yielded approximately £17,000 for the Foundation. The local authorities' contribution was increased at this time by £60,500 to assist the Foundation to maintain its programme of work during a period of high inflation. Nevertheless, it was just a year later (and following the winning of a major contract) that a far more optimistic note could be sounded with the assertion that 'There is ample justification for claiming that the year under review [1976–77] was one of the most successful in the Foundation's history… there can have been few [years] during which the available resources have been used to better effect.'

A more positive feature of 1974–75 was the decision to invite each LEA to nominate a Liaison Officer. It was reported that 'almost all the authorities have responded to this invitation, many of them enthusiastically'. It was hoped to use these LEA personnel as a channel of communication between the members and the Foundation: regional conferences were planned during which their views on the NFER's future work programme would be sought. The practice started this year, and continued for some years thereafter, of listing the names of these LEA Liaison Officers in an appendix to the Annual Report. Many of these Liaison Officers were described as Chief or Principal Advisers, but a gamut of job titles are recorded, from Research Assistant to Director of Education. A number of those links proceeded, in time, to become the chief officers in various education departments around the country.

The 30th Annual Report for 1975–76 included opaque references to 'a development which could have far-reaching consequences for the future of the Foundation' with a working party constituted to examine the possibility of a close working relationship between the Schools Council and the NFER. This working party had

> *strongly affirmed the need for the Council to continue its practice of ear-marking a part of its 'future starts programme' for work to be commissioned on the Foundation. This is particularly welcome since one of our major problems stems from the fact that the size of the Foundation's research programme is indeterminate. This has been the case since the 1960s when we first began to accept funds for sponsored projects. The income obtained from sponsoring organisations is variable and unpredictable and consequently the size and composition of the staff we need for carrying out research and for providing the necessary ancillary services – administrative, accounting, information, data processing and statistics – cannot be accurately forecast from year to year.*

(NFER Annual Report, 1975–76)

By the next year, however, the concordat planned with the Schools Council, which would have facilitated forward planning, had encountered a setback due to the Council's own uncertainty about its funds and a review of its structure. Yates' comments at this time encapsulated the conundrum which was experienced during much of the Foundation's history, namely that its managers could not anticipate from one year to the next what support might be forthcoming with all the attendant insecurities which this situation presented.

The policy of acknowledging through the Honours List the contribution made to society by educationalists was well-established, as will have been noted from the array of knighted individuals who had played an important role in the first half of the Foundation's history. There was explicit reference to this when Yates congratulated Mr L. W. K. Brown – recently retired as Education Officer of the Association of County Councils, and who was the Vice-Chairman of the Foundation's Board and Chairman of the Finance and General Purposes Sub-Committee – on the award of a CBE in the 1976 Queen's Birthday Honours List. The Director wryly observed that: 'Since scarcely a year passes without a member of the Board being featured in the Honours List it can be claimed that there is a high correlation between service on the Board and the award of distinctions of this kind. That a causal relationship can be inferred from this association is a hypothesis that has not yet been disconfirmed.'

Chapter 6

Expanding Challenges
1976–1982

The 1976–77 Annual Report contained confirmation of a vitally important, long-term contract won by the NFER. Following two DES-sponsored, ground-breaking feasibility studies in developing and using banks of questions for assessing pupil attainments in mathematics, the Foundation was entrusted with a significant share in the monitoring of national standards of attainment programme (Sumner, 1975). This was a programme that was being developed by the Assessment of Performance Unit (APU), jointly funded by the DES and the Welsh Office. These were to be the largest group of projects that the Foundation had ever undertaken, involving work of enormous scope and complexity under the leadership of Dr Clare Burstall. The work of the APU was seen by some as heralding the beginning of political intervention into the world of educational standards.

> *An Assessment of Performance Unit… [began]…to formulate models of different segments of the curriculum and ways in which samples of pupils throughout the country could provide policy-makers with information about the standards reached. Terror strikes easily in the educational establishment's breasts and this creation, together with some statements that seemed to lay the inefficiencies of the British economy at the feet of the schools, were thought to mean that the DES might take up a prescriptive role on standards. In fact, the Assessment of Performance Unit was not to concern itself with individual schools or individual authorities, but was to provide information on performance about the whole system and lead thinking on a common curriculum core.*
>
> (Kogan, 1978:65)

Monitoring Performance in Mathematics began in April 1977 and a parallel project, *Monitoring Performance in Language*, was planned for 1979. The special problems of Wales were taken account of with the *Development of Assessment Materials in the Welsh Language* project. The Director welcomed the work being undertaken in the development of assessment materials in the Welsh language, recognising that it had been '…a matter of concern that Wales has figured rather more prominently in our title than in our programme of activities…this omission is now being remedied'.

A further significant development in the Foundation's support services was the creation of the Monitoring Services Unit (MSU). The Unit was set up in April 1977 to coordinate and provide administrative and technical services for the teams responsible for the monitoring of standards in mathematics and language. The DES decided to utilise this unit as a central agency to provide support for all the monitoring exercises that the Assessment of Performance Unit was to superintend in mathematics, language and science in England, Wales and Northern Ireland. The MSU's responsibilities included liaison with the schools involved in the testing programmes each year, and the establishment, for research purposes, of a record-keeping and information retrieval system for schools in England and Wales. The Unit's work embraced all the contacts that were necessary with local education authorities and schools to secure appropriate samples for national monitoring, and the supervision and organisation of the administrative arrangements for testing. It also kept a research register of schools which were participating in the Foundation's testing and research programmes in order to avoid overburdening particular schools. The MSU's work in the first 12 months of its existence included the planning and preparation of administering the testing programmes and pilot testing involving over 10,000 pupils in 185 schools on behalf of the Mathematics and Language Monitoring Teams. In order to ensure that the agreed policy of pupil anonymity was maintained, the Unit had had to incorporate a system of pupil reference numbers in its administrative procedures.

Following approaches made by many local education authorities, the Foundation decided to embark on the development of an Item Banking Service for use by authorities and schools (see the definition of an 'item bank' on page 53). It was stated at the time that: 'A developed item bank will enable those who wish to use tests for monitoring or other purposes to compile tests that specifically suit their requirements…It is intended that the instruments made available by this means will be, in many respects, similar to those used in the national monitoring projects and that eventually the two systems will be so related as to permit local users to interpret their results in terms of national standards.'

In response to the requirements of the Education Act 1976, which placed a duty on LEAs to cater for handicapped pupils in ordinary schools unless certain difficulties prevailed, an important DES-sponsored project, *The Education of Handicapped Children in Ordinary Schools*, began in September 1977 under Dr Seamus Hegarty, then a Senior Research Officer. Carried out in cooperation with 14 education authorities, this project – scheduled for completion in August 1980 – was to evaluate the various schemes of integration that were then in operation.

The Department had also commissioned the Foundation to carry out *An Evaluation of Pilot Schemes for Unified Vocational Preparation*, looking at the courses designed to combine training for the specific skills required for a particular occupation with the development of those more general skills needed to equip young people for adult life. Yates saw the major emphasis of the Foundation's areas of research – the assessment of performance, the educational provision for handicapped pupils and students, and issues associated with the education of pupils between the ages of 16 and 19, particularly in further education – as evidence of the Foundation's responsiveness to the major preoccupations of its members' interests. The Calouste Gulbenkian Foundation invited the NFER's cooperation in an inquiry into the teaching of dance in schools which covered Scotland as well as England and Wales. The Information Division reported at this time that there was a growing acknowledgement of the linkage between those involved in education and in social services departments and agencies.

The publication of the *Register of Educational Research* – for which a feasibility study had first been funded by the DES and the Social Science Research Council in September 1973 – took place in December 1976 and contained information on 2,200 projects. *The Register of Educational Research in the United Kingdom 1973–76* was described as 'the first essay in computer-based publishing and the first issue of an annual standard work of reference' by the NFER Publishing Company.

About two-thirds of the Foundation's income in 1976–77 came from sponsored research while LEA subscriptions that year amounted to £238,445. The NFER Publishing Company, which had now moved into new premises at Darville House in the centre of Windsor, enjoyed a significant increase in turnover to £781,496, with £127,182 of that income made over to the Foundation. The Publishing Company's main test publishing venture was the *British Ability Scales*, which covered the age range $2^1/_2$ to 17 years and were described as 'the first tests of individual mental ability in the world to utilize Rasch item scaling and as such they represent a unique publishing venture for the Company'.

Articles submitted for the Foundation's journal, *Educational Research*, had continued to arrive at the rate of about 140 a year. A quarter of these were accepted and those rejected were 'always accompanied by a reason and, where possible, a critique of the material, compiled with the help of referees in the Foundation's projects – a not unimportant form of liaison between the Foundation and other educational researchers'.

Dr Clare Burstall became Head of the Research Division as well as a Deputy Director. John Fox was now described as the Deputy Director (Financial, Legal, Committee, Secretarial and Administrative Services). Jim Davies headed the Information Division and the list of Principal Research Officers now consisted of Bruce Choppin, Philip Clift, Derek Foxman, Tom Gorman, Anthony James, Malcolm Parlett, Margaret Reid, Ray Sumner and Alan Willmott.

In pursuance of Yates' intention to improve dissemination, the Board of Management gave its approval to a new series of publications designated as *Research in Progress*. These were to be produced by the Foundation itself rather than by the Publishing Company and distributed free to member organisations. They were designed to provide interim reports of research projects still in progress and notification of preliminary findings, as well as to provide a means of reporting results that were incidental to the major purposes of an inquiry – 'spin-offs', as they were described – and which yet could be of considerable interest to members and other researchers.

A significant enlargement of the Information Division's role came about in 1977–78. Ministers representing the nine countries which were members of what was then the European Economic Community recommended that a network of national centres should be established to collect and exchange information relating to educational policy issues at both the national and local level. A feasibility study was financed by the DES, and George Cooke, the recently retired Chief Education Officer for Lincolnshire, assisted in a consultative capacity to enable the Foundation to establish such a national information centre, which was called EPIC, an acronym for the Education Policy Information Centre. Janet May was appointed as the first EPIC Project Leader when it began its work in April 1978 as part of a network that became known as EURYDICE (not an acronym, but the name adopted for this European network from the Greek mythological figure) in 1980. It was intended to provide a means for the exchange of information between the European partners on educational issues of common interest. It was also planned at that time that the Centre would act as a central information link for the English and Welsh local education authorities and a pilot activity was carried out with a number of LEAs to that end. It was reported that considerable interest was shown by both the education sector and other organisations in the establishment of this Centre and the links it was making with our European partners.

During 1977–78, the Foundation's income continued to rise, especially from sponsored research and from the Publishing Company, and that year exceeded one million pounds for the first time with an average of 112 staff employed. The NFER Publishing Company's report records that the company, previously a 'minor adjunct to the Foundation', now 'stands securely on its own firm base, and has acquired a reputation which equals that of many long established publishing houses...The production and distribution of the Foundation's research reports – once its sole *raison d'être* – is now only a minor part of its total activity'. By then the company produced some 30 or so new titles a year and had an extensive booklist, with its marketing and sales activities being extended well beyond Europe. The NFER had also acquired a residual interest in the National Institute of Industrial Psychology's books and tests, which were also to be handled by the Publishing Company.

The Test Department's activities had also grown spectacularly in scope and size, performing as the agency for a large proportion of the tests imported into this country from the USA. Its success was largely attributed to the maintenance of a sizeable research and development department and an advisory service which helped it to match its products to the clients' needs. Publication of the *Register of Educational Research* and the agreement with the Council of Europe to publish the *EUDISED R&D Bulletin*, to appear in four editions per annum, had also placed the Company in a key position as a European disseminator of educational research information and complemented the EPIC project that was being developed within the Foundation's Information Division. The Company's publications had been featured in more than 50 exhibitions at home and overseas, including the Toronto Conference of the American Educational Research Association in March 1978. Importantly, the Company was also aware of the potential of the industrial sector, despite the reported scepticism of industry at the time about the use of tests. The previously neglected school/work interface was also now being targeted, with tests being produced for apprentices and the clerical work sector.

Mark Carlisle succeeded Shirley Williams as the NFER's President in June 1979. An important funding development took place when the Foundation underwent scrutiny in the summer and autumn of 1978 by the local authorities as part of an exercise undertaken to determine which national bodies should continue to receive financial support under Section 2 (7) of the Local Government Act, 1974. The outcome proved favourable and the funding arrangements for the NFER were confirmed. The amount of commissioned research had increased to a figure of £519,000 in the year ending 31 March 1979, as compared to the previous year's best record of £335,000. The Foundation's very success was, however, again causing problems in accommodating the range of staff needed to provide its services to sponsors, and additional accommodation had to be rented in Slough. Eight new projects were finished, and eight started, during 1979–80. A new sponsoring body, the Transport and Road Research Laboratory, funded an investigation into the use of video-recording in road safety teaching in primary schools.

In his introduction to the 1978–79 Annual Report, Yates commented on the issue of the short-term contracts offered to staff, which caused them – and the Foundation as an employer – concern. An informal inquiry had been held into the subsequent careers of a sample of staff members who had left the Foundation after completing their contracts. This revealed that six former staff who had been initially appointed to relatively junior posts in the NFER were by then occupying University Chairs in Education; one ex-employee was the Deputy Principal of a polytechnic and another the Principal of a college of higher education. A staff member who had been in publishing had become the head of a successful firm of management consultants. At least 12 others were known to be occupying academic posts in universities and polytechnics, some at Reader and Senior Lecturer levels. A similar number were employed in a variety of local education authority posts. And one former member of the NFER staff had achieved what the Director described as 'perhaps the final accolade' of becoming a member of Her Majesty's Inspectorate. This information was provided, it was stated, in the hope that it might 'possibly [be] of some comfort' to the current staff on their limited-term contracts and to demonstrate that successful service with the Foundation could 'lead to interesting and responsible positions in various parts of the education service'.

Four staff members were being supported this year on PhD courses under the Foundation's Education and Training Scheme from which £1,100 had been paid in grants.

The establishment of the first of the Foundation's regional offices took place when Dr Eurwen Price was appointed to direct the Welsh Office-funded *Development of Assessment Materials in the Welsh Language*. Dr Price, who headed the Foundation's office in Wales from its formation in 1978 until 1990, has recounted that a government Minister was on his feet in the House of Commons announcing the start of the APU monitoring of performance programme when one of the Members of Parliament from Wales asked him if performance in Welsh was to be monitored in Welsh schools. Apparently, this had not even been considered by the DES, but the Minister replied off the top of his head that Welsh would, of course, be one of the subjects monitored in Wales. This inadvertent commitment was passed on to the government's Welsh Office, who turned to the NFER for assistance. The Foundation then approached Dr Eurwen Price and appointed her as a Research Consultant in September 1976 to direct the monitoring project. At first, she worked part-time and from home until, in 1978, a work centre was based in the Department of Education at University College, Swansea, with Dr Price being assisted by two researchers, one of whom, Robat Powell, succeeded Dr Price after her retirement in 1990 as the Head of the Welsh Office. Robat Powell achieved national acclaim in Wales when he was awarded the Bardic Chair at the National Eisteddfod in 1985, being the first non-native Welsh speaker to achieve this literary feat. The NFER Welsh Office (or, in Welsh, Sefydliad Cenedlaethol er Ymchwil i Addysg and its acronym of 'SCYA') was thus born.

Dr Eurwen Price, Founder and Head of the Welsh Office until 1990

The Financial Report for 1978–79 indicated that sponsored income rose by 54 per cent and the group turnover was now £1.23 million, the amount of sponsored research having by then doubled in the course of the previous six years. There was an average number of 127 employees that year with staff remuneration recorded to be £564,327. This Annual Report revealed that one Foundation employee's salary – no doubt that of the Director – was paid at a figure of between £12,500 and £15,000, while two others were earning between £10,000 and £12,500.

Statistical Services now returned to The Mere after many years in Erin House in Slough's High Street and a capital fund was set up in anticipation of new premises to replace expensively rented temporary accommodation. Online literature searches by the Information Services had become well established and this facility was also being provided on a cost-recovery basis to other organisations. Volume III of the *Register of Educational Research* was published in 1978 and *Educational Research* continued at three issues per year.

Yates sounded a sombre warning note, however. There had been an agreement, operative for nearly ten years, that the cost of the Foundation's services in real terms should remain at a constant level and that any increase in the size of the grant sought from the local education authorities should be restricted to such amounts as were required to meet the costs of inflation (the so-called 'plateau principle'). As LEAs were being compelled to cut their own levels of expenditure, the Foundation would inevitably have to share in those reductions. Some proposed research had, therefore, been shelved. Additionally, a decrease could be seen in the amount of covenanted money received from the Publishing Company's profits which had provided a sizeable addition to the basic income, as publishers were also experiencing the financial pinch from reduced public expenditure. Even so, the 'British Ability Scales' had proved a major publishing success and sales of £70,000 had been reached in only four months. The Publishing Company's purchasing department were thanked for having searched out a 'quite weird variety of toys, building blocks and even smooth, $2^1/2$ inch long stones' for inclusion in these test kits.

Sir Edward Britton, a previous Chairman of the Finance and General Purposes Committee, joined the ranks of the Foundation's all-knighted list of Vice-Presidents in October 1979. However, one of that newly augmented quartet, Sir Francis Hill, died in January 1980.

Some internal reorganisation now took place with all research relating to testing and development brought together under the general direction of Dr Bruce Choppin. Choppin had acquired an international reputation as a psychometrist and was a recognised authority on item banking. Also, a Local Research Consultancy Service was set up under Dr Ray Sumner to lend technical support to those who were willing to carry out investigations on their own behalf. In this way, the Foundation was able to offer its expert help and advice to local studies that member organisations intended to pursue.

The Department of Education and Science was by now far the most prominent sponsor of research at the Foundation. As the Director pointed out, such commissioned research both coincided very often with the issues of crucial interest to the Foundation's own members and helped to maintain a much higher level of support services at the NFER than would otherwise have been possible. The largest sponsored undertaking in the Foundation was now the work being carried out on behalf of the APU monitoring performance in mathematics and language in schools in England, Wales and Northern Ireland. Of the NFER's own projects, the largest was concerned with the Local Education Authorities and Schools Item Bank (LEASIB), which would enable local authorities – and, eventually, individual schools – to acquire tests that were designed to meet specific requirements. Despite this range of developments, substantial sums had had to be transferred from the reserves to cover deficits in the Foundation's finances in 1979–1980, with staff remuneration having by then risen to £819,366 for an average of 140 employees.

There was the first mention at this time of short-scale commissions, involving little notice and then intense research activity over a few months to meet the needs of the sponsor. 'There are indications that there could well be more invitations to respond fairly rapidly to requirements of this kind', wrote the Director, prophetically. He also warned that this cut across what had been the normal pattern of allocating staff to full-time assignments and required more flexible staffing patterns to help the Foundation adapt to these new developments. This was indeed a harbinger of the pattern of things to come for the Foundation.

The time that elapsed between the end of a project and the appearance of a published report of its findings was recognised as a problem in the dissemination of the Foundation's research. In addition to improving the general performance in this regard, it was intended to 'encourage the practice of producing homespun interim reports, regular newsletters and other means of conveying the results of our investigations to our members with the minimum of delay'.

George Cooke, who established the two information services, EMIE and EURYDICE, at the NFER

Following the establishment of the Education Policy Information Centre (EPIC) at the Foundation, it was felt that the education authorities in this country might similarly benefit from an information service dedicated to their needs. A joint proposal was successfully submitted to the DES by the Society of Education Officers and the NFER and, in January 1981, the Project for the Exchange of Management Information on Educational Policy and Practice was launched.[1] David Streatfield was appointed as the Project Leader to run this new information service for the LEAs with George Cooke, who was by then the General Secretary to the Society of Education Officers, acting as the project's principal adviser. Thirty LEAs took part in a pilot to provide policy information on six themes which were selected by the LEAs themselves as having important implications for their operations at that time, *viz.* the transition from school to work; falling school rolls and the management of contraction; the induction and in-service training of teachers; the educational implications of micro-technology (*sic*); the assessment of pupil performance; and the implementation of Health and Safety at Work legislation in educational establishments. Yates predicted that EMIE '…could well develop into one of the most valuable services that the Foundation has to offer' and in April 1982 EMIE was launched nationally following its successful experimental phase.

The 35th Annual Report for 1980–81 recorded that the DES's Assessment of Performance Unit had asked the Foundation to monitor standards in French, German and Spanish, with the Welsh Office also commissioning further work on the development of assessment materials in Welsh. The DES had also commissioned the NFER to study special educational provision within the further education sector. A critical review on the education of West Indian children had been produced for the Rampton Committee and the Foundation was to follow this up with a comparable report dealing with other ethnic groups. 'This evidence, indicating that our regular sponsors are inclined to return, cash in hand, serves to demonstrate that the Foundation's researchers are producing work that is both of a satisfactory quality and relevant to the needs of policy makers and practitioners', wrote the Director. An additional sponsor had been attracted this year, the Department of Health and Social Security, which had commissioned the Foundation to carry out an evaluation of training courses for hearing therapists. In all, 30 research projects were being undertaken that year and commissioned research amounted to £1,100,650, an increase of about 30 per cent on the previous year. The Director could now observe that 'We have been complimented particularly on the extent to which we are succeeding in furnishing reports that are clearly written, jargon-free accounts of the research undertaken but which nevertheless do full justice to the complexity of the design and analysis of the findings.'

A major controversy rocked the Foundation's work in assessment, particularly that of the APU teams, in this period. The use of the 'Rasch modelling method' – which sought to apply statistical allowances to the changes that would occur in measurement testing over time – had aroused strong opposition in some quarters. It was decided that the use of this method should be dropped by the Foundation's researchers after pressure from sponsors. Professor Harvey Goldstein, an opponent of the Rasch technique, was then appointed as a consultant to the Foundation on statistical matters. Amongst those on the NFER's research staff who were unhappy with this decision, Dr Bruce Choppin, who was at the centre of this controversy, was one of a number who decided to leave the Foundation. This outstanding researcher was later to lose his life while en route to take up a post abroad.[2]

The Foundation has always been dependent on the support of a range of individuals in the wider world of education and this year special thanks were expressed to George Cooke, both for his work with the fledgling Education Management Information Exchange and for acting as a consultant on provision for children with special educational needs, a subject on which he had expert insight having served as the Vice-Chairman of the Warnock Committee of Inquiry. Peter Coles of the Association of County Councils had also assisted in a comprehensive review of the Foundation staff's conditions of service this year. The award of a CBE to Angela Rumbold, a local politician representing the Association of Metropolitan Authorities on the Board of Management (and who later became a Minister in the DES), was also reported.

Internally, a number of special units had been created. Reference has already been made to the Local Research Consultancy Service which was set up in April 1980 to provide a wide range of services to schools and LEAs. Another important development was the creation of a separate Computer Services Unit in January 1981 to provide a data processing service to the Foundation and to other users. Danesh Omrani, a former computer consultant to the Iranian government and head of a college Computer Science department in a Tehran college, was appointed as the Computer Manager with Doreen Trinder as the Unit's Operations Manager. The Foundation's Test Services were set up following a reorganisation, taking over the major commitment to the Local Education Authorities and Schools Item Bank.

Extra expenditure had been incurred from the 1980–81 budget due to the completion of more new accommodation, the Library Block extension having cost £124,047, plus the cost of new computing facilities. This meant that the Foundation had once again to draw on its reserves to avoid a deficit. There was an average of 158 employees during this period and the cost of staff remuneration topped the £1 million mark for the first time.

A major development which had a profound effect on future income was the formation of the NFER-NELSON Publishing Company, jointly owned by the Foundation and a commercial firm, Thomas Nelson and Sons Ltd. On 14 January 1981, the new company took on the trading operations, and the publication of educational and psychological tests and books, from the NFER Publishing Company. (The latter ceased to trade but thereafter acted as a holding company providing management services.) The jointly owned publishing operation introduced a new commercial expertise and rigour to the Foundation's activities in this area.

The 36th Annual Report for 1981–82 indicated that the post of Foundation President was vacant. Sir Keith Joseph's occupancy of the post of Secretary of State for Education and Science (from 1981–1986) brought to an end the tradition of having the holder of this government office as the Foundation's President. Unconventional in this, as in so many other ways, Joseph ceased to follow the practice of his predecessors.[4] After a lacuna of two years when this office remained vacant, the NFER would henceforth no longer have the government's education minister as its honorary figurehead. In the light of the increasing politicisation of the education debate during the time of this Conservative administration, this was a traditional appointment that would, in any case, have become inappropriate.

The Director wrote of 'far from favourable circumstances' this year but income still rose again to £1,170,516. Seventeen reports were published with 11 more near to completion. Improvements had been made in the publication and dissemination of research findings, with shorter intervals between the completion of research and the emergence of the final report. NFER-NELSON was reported to be 'serving us admirably in ensuring that they [i.e. reports] are expeditiously produced and in an attractive format'.

The Board of Management undertook a review of the NFER's activities for the next triennium as well as a review of staff conditions of service. Now that the Foundation had decided to acquire its own central computing facility, a new IBM 4331 computer was installed. Another development was the formation of the Test and Research Advisory Service, which was formed from the amalgamation of Test Services and the Local Research Consultancy Service. Within Information Services, a Graphics Department had been formed from the Exhibitions Department.

With financial losses having been incurred in the two previous years, a major review of the Foundation's financial position was undertaken during the latter part of 1981–82. While the income from the local authorities had been increased in line with inflation, a cut of two per cent in real terms was experienced. Their grant was fixed at £300,000 – 'about £117,000 below the level which might have been expected'. £346,909 had to be brought in from the reserves to redress the adverse financial position. This was a matter of great concern with a major reduction in research and services for the membership envisaged if the position was not rectified. George Low, editor of the *Education Journal*, has identified 1980–1983 as a period when the political leadership of CLEA (the Council of Local Education Authorities) was attempting 'to bring financial discipline and a market approach on the quangos…and to [produce] a steady reduction in central funding to encourage the NFER to become more market-orientated'.[3] This was a time of financial stringency that was only reversed when the party political control of CLEA changed and a seven per cent increase was granted to the Foundation in 1983–84.

Notes

[1]   Sumner relates his involvement with others, including Dr Brian Wilcox, Chief Adviser at Sheffield LEA, in launching this information service. Sir James Hamilton, the Permanent Under-Secretary of State at the DES, who later became the Foundation's President, had also been influential in EMIE's establishment through his urging the LEAs to share information on good policies and practice (Sumner, 1996).

[2]   A defence of Choppin's work is presented in Linacre, J. (1995). 'Bruce Choppin: Visionary', Rasch Measurement Transactions, 8, 4, 394: this article was reproduced in the NFER Newsletter, 40, October 1997. See also Sumner, where he provides a personal observation on this controversy (Sumner, 1996:25).

[3]   From a private letter from George Low to Ralph Tabberer, 26 June 1996.

[4]   'Joseph, one of the most interesting and constructive politicians ever to head the Education Ministry, was genuinely opposed to taking legislative powers to give "the holder of my Office" complete control of the content of education, because he shared the view which had predominated among his generation – that this would be a totalitarian move inappropriate to a democratic Britain ... he continued to hold this view, opposing the National Curriculum from the back benches in the House of Lords' (Maclure, 2000:216–17).

Chapter 7

Change and Reorganisation
1983–1990

Following Alfred Yates's retirement at the end of March 1983, the Foundation's sixth Director, Dr Clare Burstall, assumed office from 1 April, being the first woman and the first such appointment from a currently serving member of staff to take up this leadership role. The new Director, a linguist and psychologist, had spent all her working life at the Foundation, where she had taken on roles of ever greater responsibility following her time as project leader of the team evaluating the teaching of French in British primary schools. There followed a fundamental reorganisation to the senior management team when three more staff were appointed as Deputy Directors – Seamus Hegarty, Margaret Reid and Danesh Omrani, each to their different areas of responsibility – while John Fox held the title of Foundation Secretary and Deputy Director, Finance and General Administration.

Dr Clare Burstall,
Director,
1983–1993

The local authority associations had restored their grant to the Foundation to its former level for 1983–84, granting a sum of £417,000, a matter of obvious relief to the outgoing Director as 'the possibility of slipping down an inclined plane was an alarming prospect'. Yates mentions that the income of the Foundation from sponsored projects now exceeded one-and-a-quarter-million pounds as compared with the £203,000 he had reported when he first took up the Director's office in 1972. Yates expressed a conviction that the list of the Foundation's projects was demonstrably related to the practical concerns of much of the membership and that the NFER's researchers could not be accused of following their own esoteric research interests. The programme that year contained 29 research projects on a variety of issues – special needs; monitoring standards of performance; primary, secondary and further education; parental choice; transfer procedures; international research and reviews of research, as well as the work of the two information services, EMIE and EPIC. There was also a newly created Test Development Unit, set up to examine innovative approaches to educational measurement, as well as a new Membership Services section. The income of what was known as the Additional Activities Programme, derived very largely from royalties and the profits from the jointly owned NFER-NELSON Publishing Company, increased to £288,000. Twenty-one books and 25 substantial articles in *Educational Research* and other journals were published by staff members.

By the time of the 38th Annual Report for 1983–84 the two year vacancy in the office of the Foundation's President had been filled with the appointment of Sir James Hamilton. Sir James had had a distinguished career, first in aeronautical research, and later as a senior civil servant. He served as the Permanent Under-Secretary of State in the Department of Education and Science between 1976 and 1983 and then went on to give the benefit of his wide experience to the NFER and a host of other academic institutions. The number of Vice-Presidents had also been increased to five with the addition of L. W. K. Brown CBE and A. W. S. Hutchings CBE during that year. Professor William (Bill) Taylor became Chairman of the Board of Management from December 1983. His presence in that capacity renewed the historical link with the University of London Institute of Education where he had been the Director before becoming Principal of the University of London itself and, later, the Vice-Chancellor at Hull. Also in 1983, a Conservative Councillor, Judith Walpole (whose surname later changed to Chaplin), became the Board's Vice-Chairman and Chairman of the Finance and General Purposes Committee. She was regarded as a high-flier who went on to become Prime Minister John Major's political secretary. She then sat briefly as a MP before her early death. (A diary she kept of her time in the Prime Minister's office was published posthumously.) Her appointment occurred during a period when both local and central government were under the control of the same political party and a critical view was being taken of those bodies like the NFER which were in receipt of public funds.

The new Director, Dr Clare Burstall, wrote of having had to carry out 'a critical and comprehensive review of our current activities and…attempting to discern areas of priority for our future endeavours'. The circumstances under which research was commissioned were changing and she commented that:

…most external funding is won nowadays in competitive tender: that is, selected institutions are invited by a sponsor to submit research proposals in response to a detailed brief, often within a very short space of time. Those short-listed are then invited to defend their proposals face-to-face with representatives of the sponsoring body. This is a searching process and one that calls for considerable intestinal fortitude. News of success or failure follows a week or so later.

NFER Annual Report, 1983–84

Dr Burstall also commented that 'we are particularly conscious of the need to attract industry-sponsored research and to build up some standing in the area of research into the newer technologies. We are convinced that, if we are to ensure the Foundation's continuing prosperity, we must devote much of our effort to breaking into areas of research that we have not traditionally tapped.' Nevertheless, it was restated that 'our first allegiance must always be to the LEAs and to the many and urgent issues that they inevitably address: our research programme manifestly reflects our practical concern with the problems of today'.

Having no doubt that competitive tendering was now to become the dominant mode of research funding, Dr Burstall wrote of the implications for the Foundation's working ways. It would be necessary to maintain a degree of flexibility in staffing so that people could, if necessary, be redeployed at short notice to work on a new proposal; as well as to 'train staff in the subtle skills required to defend a proposal successfully'. There was also a need to maintain a keen awareness of the issues likely to generate future research so that the Foundation was prepared, when invited, to come forward with new proposals. And 'above all, we need to recognise that we will sometimes have to move very fast indeed'. To that end, a vigorous programme of staff training was to be embarked upon to equip all staff – support staff as well as researchers – with appropriate skills for the new demands of the future.

A new departmental structure had been introduced, giving greater responsibility to Heads of Department as well as 'encouraging a healthy competitiveness for the funds available to develop departmental research initiatives'. The staff had themselves been involved in working parties to formulate appropriate policies and practices for the future; in the production of training modules for the staff development programme; and advising on relevant courses and conferences for staff to attend. It was also noted that 'The introduction of a lively staff newsletter has helped to make us all aware of the impact of one another's activities on the quality of life of the Foundation'. This newsletter, appearing at varying time intervals thereafter, provided insights into the lives of those working for the Foundation, revealing unexpected and often amusing facts about its staff members. (The *NFER Newsletter*, published only for the Foundation's own staff members and written by them, should not be confused with *NFER News*, which is circulated widely and contains information on the NFER's current research and publications.)

A new Department of Information Research and Development in the field of education was set up in 1984 under David Streatfield. It incorporated both the Education Management Information Exchange and the Education Policy Information Centre information services, as well as two new initiatives, the Centre for the Evaluation of Information Technology in Education (CITE) and a project which looked at the use of information skills in schools. EMIE, which had initially been funded by the DES/Welsh Office/NFER from January 1981 until March 1985, had by now successfully demonstrated that there was a demand for the exchange of information on educational policy and practice issues amongst the LEAs it served in England and Wales. A feature of EMIE's operation was that it had its own network of link people, with one such contact nominated by each LEA, whose role was both to provide and receive information. Its staff were also supported in their work by its principal adviser, George Cooke, and an experienced team of part-time consultants, which included at that time three former Chief Education Officers, a former senior officer in the DES, and an ex-member of HMI.

The local authority support for the Membership Programme in 1983–84 amounted to £429,300 and the income from sponsors totalled £1,192,000. The Additional Activities Programme provided an income of £288,000, the same as in the previous year. One of the Deputy Directors, the long-serving John Fox, who had done so much to put the Foundation on a sound financial footing, retired in April 1984. David Bowles succeeded him as the Foundation's Acting Secretary.

By the time of the 39th Annual Report for 1984–85, Dr Burstall was able to report a 12 per cent increase on the amount of sponsored income which had been attracted that year. One of the seven new projects was a highly prestigious contract, won by the Foundation in competitive tender against formidable opposition, from a major new sponsor, the Manpower Services Commission – an executive arm of the Department of Employment – for the evaluation of the Technical and Vocational Education Initiative (TVEI) schemes.

The national evaluation of the organisation and operation of TVEI, whose Project Leader was Dr Sheila Stoney, began in January 1985. It examined a range of schemes in the 57 LEAs which had begun to implement TVEI in the two years since the Manpower Services Commission had launched this major initiative which aimed to offer young people from 14 to 18 an enhanced curriculum of a more specifically technical and vocational nature. The NFER evaluation used a wide range of quantitative and qualitative research methods in order to meet its brief. It placed a strong emphasis too on the dissemination of the research findings to different audiences within the education and training services and to working in close collaboration with local project personnel.

The TVEI evaluation, which lasted till 1989, was followed by further work in this area looking at the TVEI extension, in which Bob Stradling and Lesley Saunders played a lead role under Dr Stoney, and a four-year Cohort Study of TVEI students, led by Penelope Weston. In addition, a TVEI database was maintained by Barbara Bloomfield. The income derived from this huge evaluation enterprise, which continued until the mid-1990s, was worth several millions of pounds to the Foundation. Moreover, the success of the TVEI contracts generated a whole suite of subsequent major evaluations, such as Compacts and Training Credits, funded by the government's Education and Employment Departments. It was work which established the reputation of the NFER as one of the few research institutions that was capable of handling large, complex, mixed methodological evaluations.

The Research Programme also included a survey of expressive arts in the initial training of primary teachers. The NFER had funded a project to study the roles, management and practices of the LEA advisory services which played a crucial role in the maintenance and development of standards of teaching. A hint was given of 'promising discussions with new contacts in the world of industry', the interface between education and industry having become increasingly salient.

The Director spoke again of the heavy investment given to increasing staff development opportunities and managerial skills. While the Foundation was unable to recognise staff efforts above and beyond the call of duty with tangible perks, the Director had instituted 'achievement lunches' for staff who had made a significant contribution to the life of the organisation. A successful Open Day was also held during this year to publicise the work of the NFER.

In February 1984, the Foundation took over the compilation of a Register of Research into Special Education, begun at the University of London Institute of Education, with funding from the Economic and Social Research Council.

The Test Development Unit continued to produce new assessment material for publication by NFER-NELSON as well as investigating more experimental forms of assessment. In the course of its work in both developing tests for LEAs and advising on their use, item banks had been created in four areas; mathematics, verbal reasoning, reading comprehension, and non-verbal reasoning.

Income from sponsors in 1984–85 was £1,341,000, an increase of 12.5 per cent over the previous year's figure of £1,192,000. The Additional Activities Programme provided a figure of £387,000 which funded the development of new tests and research projects whose costs could not have been met from within the funds available to the Membership Programme.

During this year, the Foundation received a generous bequest of £168,000, plus accrued interest, from the estate of the late Dr Ian MacFarlane Smith, a former member of the Foundation staff, which was to be used for work in the development of spatial ability and other modes of right-hemisphere thinking. These funds continued to be applied for these purposes up until all the legacy was spent in 1996. Dr MacFarlane Smith also bequeathed to the Foundation a large collection of books and papers. Amongst these was a full record of his dreams over a period of 50 years (1932–1982), which he had collected with the intention that they might be studied for their potential educational, therapeutic and prognostic value.

It was not until the 40th Annual Report for 1985–86 that photographs first made their appearance in this publication. In January 1986, Mrs Nicole Harrison, who had chaired the Association of Metropolitan Authorities, became the Board's Vice-Chairman. Sir Ronald Gould stood down as one of the Foundation's Vice-Presidents in April. Dr Seamus Hegarty was appointed to the newly established post of Senior Deputy Director and Dick Weindling was appointed the Head of a new Department of Educational Management and Professional Skills, which was to have but a short life.

Funding from industry had been attracted for the first time in the Foundation's history to set up a new information agency named BRIEF (Briefing Service for Industry on Education), modelled on the successful Education Management Information Exchange. It came into being as a result of a National Economic Development Office initiative and had the support of both the Confederation of British Industry and the Trades Union Congress. BRIEF began in the autumn of 1986 and was financed by grants from the DES, the Department of Trade and Industry and the Manpower Services Commission, as well as donations from many industrial companies. Another first was achieved when a manager from industry, David Barnett, was seconded from the BP (British Petroleum) company to supervise the development of this service, whose purpose was to meet the needs of those in industry and commerce for information on educational topics. The Director wrote that 'We feel extremely encouraged by this development, which underlines our determination to move away from the narrowly-school centred image that the Foundation's name still evokes in certain quarters and to increase the number and variety of our sponsors, despite the difficult economic circumstances that we find ourselves in at present.'

New project monitoring systems had now been set in place, together with an annual review of the Foundation's work as a whole. New training modules too had been produced for staff development in essential areas of research expertise and a 'personnel exchange scheme' with overseas research institutes was reported to have been in operation.

Sponsored research in 1985–86 amounted to £1,386,000, an increase of 3.4 per cent over the previous year's figure. Detailed accounts of most current projects were now to be found in a new series of 'Research Sheets' that were made available to interested parties. Special needs projects continued to be prominent with seven of the research projects undertaken during this year in this category. The DES sponsored a survey on LEAs' policies and practices relating to drugs education and drugs misuse.

The Director made reference in the 1986–87 Annual Report to the *Memorandum of Association*, which defined the *raison d'être* of the Foundation.

The *Memorandum* and *Articles of Association* define the objectives of the organisation and constitution of the Foundation's governing body. The NFER is licensed as a limited company under the Companies Act 1948 and succeeding legislation. Various amendments have subsequently been made to the *Articles* since they were originally framed in 1967.

The objectives in the *Memorandum* included to 'conduct research in all or any matters affecting education'; to disseminate the results of its own researches and those carried out by others; to make a full contribution to international research; to act in an advisory capacity to government departments, LEAs and others; to serve as a vehicle for the interchange of educational ideas; organising and conducting courses and conferences; developing standardised tests as required; and maintaining a regular flow of information on educational issues. Dr Burstall saw opportunities for expansion in each of the three main areas of activity: research; the provision of courses, conferences and consultancy services; and dissemination.

The Director commented again on the 'fiercely competitive climate' with limited research funding in which the Foundation had to 'fight very hard to maintain our competitive edge'. She wrote that the Foundation had 'managed to move in recent years from a position of near-total dependence on a single sponsor to a much healthier situation in which we have been able to establish a good reputation with a number of major funding bodies, but much remains to be done... we must continue to attract new sponsors'.

The Membership Programme, financed primarily by the grant received under what was then Section 56(9) of the 1980 Local Government Planning and Land Act, now represented about a quarter of the Foundation's income. This year the submission to CLEA was oriented towards funding people rather than projects so that part of the researchers' time could be used towards the development of future research.

The Additional Activities Programme, funded largely by the income received from NFER-NELSON, principally supported the Test Development Unit. Its role was described as one in which it 'undertakes the updating and revision of existing tests, the adaptation and standardization of imported test material, and the development of new forms of assessment in what is a rapidly changing field, very much affected by advances in technology. It also responds to requests from individual LEAs to produce tests tailor-made for given purposes and has been successful in attracting a considerable amount of external funding… this unit is admirably serving its purpose and represents an area of traditional strength at the Foundation which commands wide respect.' Dr Burstall far-sightedly observed that 'there is considerable scope for expansion in the whole area of assessment and that the Foundation should be alert to respond to new opportunities, whether at local or national level'. The Director also commented that: 'At the international level, the Foundation has contributed a small part of its efforts to research of an international nature since the early 1960s, sometimes with external funding but, more frequently, using its own resources. There is currently a renewal of interest in international research, at home and abroad and this could well be an area of potential growth.'

A new Department of External Relations, headed by Dr Ray Sumner with Marilyn Farndell, who was also Personal Assistant to the Director, as his Deputy, brought together a range of previously uncoordinated expertise from various parts of the Foundation to form a coherent unit which embarked upon a programme of conferences, workshops and seminars. The Director commented that 'the whole field of in-service training is one in which the Foundation could play a much more salient role… we are also being asked, with increasing frequency, to provide consultancy services, particularly to individual LEAs'. Bob Wellburn was appointed to the post of Computer Manager, overseeing a period when computer technology would impact on every part of the Foundation.

External Relations Department staff, 1980s.
Those pictured on the right, next to the seated Dr Sumner (Tim Wright, Wendy Crees and David Upton) each worked over 25 years at the NFER

The year 1987 marked the centenary of the building of The Mere, the mansion in Slough which had become the NFER's headquarters. An exhibition was mounted of old photographs and items associated with The Mere, which was attended by a number of local people who had been involved in some way with the mansion from the days of its family occupants, including Rosalind Bentley, the niece of the late Mrs Lucy Bentley. A brief history of the building, illustrated with early photographs of The Mere and the Bentley family members, was also published that year (Griffiths, 1987). This has continued to be made available in reprinted editions to those who visit the Foundation's impressive headquarters, and to new staff members, providing information about the history of the building and its former owners (see Appendix 1). Sadly, the fierce storms of October 1987 which swept southern England brought down some fine, old trees that had graced The Mere's grounds.

The research programme reflected the diversity of work that the NFER was undertaking. It included a study of the role of the LEA Instrumental Music Service, initiated in January 1986, and an evaluation of the work of artists in schools which began in February 1987. Most importantly, the Foundation was now commissioned to conduct the national evaluation of the Lower Attaining Pupils Programme (LAPP). The 'long tail' of underachieving pupils in the country had been identified as an area of particular concern and LAPP, introduced by Sir Keith Joseph to counter this problem, was probably the first curriculum change initiative to be managed directly by the DES. The evaluation, led by Penelope Weston, and in which 17 LEAs participated, also brought about the creation of the Foundation's Northern Office.

Towards the end of the first phase of the LAPP evaluation, Dr John Harland, who had led a team of three staff from an office in Sheffield Polytechnic working on this project, suggested a Northern Office be established to act as a base for carrying out NFER research and fieldwork in the north of England. Dr Burstall and the Head of the Department in which LAPP was located, Margaret Reid, backed the proposal, which they saw would help to counter the perception in some quarters that the Foundation was largely a London and Home Counties-based organisation. They appreciated that, supplementing the already-established Welsh Office, a regional office in the north would increase the Foundation's presence there and demonstrate the NFER's commitment to providing research services across all the LEAs and schools in England and Wales.

Dr Harland was invited to put his proposal to the Board and he submitted two options: one for offices to remain in Sheffield and another for a base at the University of York. The latter was chosen, both because of York's good communication and travel connections, and because of the strong support for the idea from the University of York's Education Department, led by Professor Ian Lister. Hence, the three researchers decamped from Sheffield to new offices in Langwith College at the University of

Dr John Harland, Founder and Head of the Northern Office

York in September 1986. Things did not get off to an auspicious start, with two of the three northern pioneers, and their first secretary, leaving soon afterwards. New contracts proved difficult to find and IT communications with Slough repeatedly failed. However, in these early years, Professor Lister and Norman Rea, the Provost of Langwith College, were highly supportive of the NFER's presence within York University and helped to broker initial contacts with important sponsors. New research and support staff were also taken on and provided the necessary stability after this vulnerable beginning.

There was a healthy financial position in 1986–87. The Membership Programme amounted to £579,660, as compared to £464,850 in 1985–86. The Sponsored Research Programme was £1,603,000, an increase of 15.7 per cent over the 1985–86 figure of £1,386,000 and the Additional Activities Programme was £504,000 (in 1985–86 it had stood at £379,000). By the time of the next Annual Report for 1987–88, the Director could declare that during the first six months of 1988 the amount of externally sponsored income brought in had exceeded that for the whole of 1987 and that: 'The fastest growing area of work has undoubtedly been that of specific studies undertaken at the request of individual LEAs. These tend to be short, sharply focussed studies, often in the form of an independent evaluation of an innovatory policy or practice that the LEA has introduced...they have become many in number [although quite modestly funded] and now make a considerable contribution to our sponsored income.' The Manpower Services Commission, a major sponsor, had now been transformed into the Training Commission. Other new sponsors that year included the Economic and Social Research Council, the National Audit Office, the European Council and the Council of Europe.

Dr Burstall commented once more on the tight deadlines which now characterised the tendering process for many research contracts. Each required a fully costed proposal to be submitted within a short space of time, 'a situation which taxes our resources to the utmost and requires both research staff and those in supporting services to respond with alacrity and commitment above and beyond the normal call of duty', a response for which she gave high praise to her staff.

There had been a reorganisation of the senior management structure, with an enlarged Senior Management Team and research projects regrouped within five new and considerably larger departments, *viz.* Assessment and Measurement; Professional Studies; Evaluation and Policy Studies; Curriculum Studies; Information Research and Development. A new Centre for Research in Language and Communication had been established within the Department of Curriculum Studies, with its counterpart in Wales, and was attracting external funding.

Among other items of interest that year, it was recorded that BRIEF's pocket guide to educational acronyms and abbreviations (which could fit neatly into a Filofax) was proving a popular give-away item at meetings its staff had had with those in industry. The EMIE team, led by Valerie Gee, had benefited from the secondment of two LEA officers and a headteacher to help with the rapidly expanding work of their information service. The NFER now had a Press and Publicity Officer once again, based in the Department of External Relations. Accounting Services received well-deserved praise for the support it provided for all the Foundation's 80 projects and services, which had involved some 12,000 financial transactions. New computer equipment was helping to speed the handling of their expanding volume of work.

The Membership Programme income was £622,070 in 1987–88 and sponsored research amounted to £2,092,000, an increase of 30.5 per cent over 1986–87 but the Additional Activities Programme, at £456,000, saw a fall on the previous year's figure.

By 1988–89, NFER's work programme reflected the significant changes that were taking place in the world of education with the Education Reform Act of 1988 and the legislated National Curriculum. Professor (later, Lord) Brian Griffiths, who headed Prime Minister Margaret Thatcher's Downing Street

Policy Unit, and had considerable influence over legislative changes to education at this time, paid a visit to the NFER's Slough headquarters, recognising the part the Foundation was playing in the new assessment regime that was being introduced (Taylor, 1995: 160–84).

Clare Burstall comments once again in the 43rd Annual Report on the fierce competition and stringent conditions involved in tendering for contracts: 'One Monday morning, we received an invitation to bid for a major project in an area of interest: the finished proposal had to be with the sponsor by the Friday of the same week. And, yes, we did it, but only thanks to the magic of the Fax machine!' Sponsored income had increased by another ten per cent this year. As well as established sponsors, like the DES and the Training Agency, two most welcome newcomers this year were the School Examinations and Assessment Council (SEAC) and the National Curriculum Council (NCC). These last two were crucial gains as the Foundation experienced the phasing out of what had been its long-running work for the DES's Assessment of Performance Unit.

Duncan Graham, the Chairman and Chief Executive of the National Curriculum Council from 1988 to 1991, was later to float the idea that the NFER might become linked in with the NCC, so close and cooperatively did he feel the two bodies had worked in the introduction of the National Curriculum.

If mergers are in the air then perhaps the place of the NFER should come under scrutiny. The council and the NFER have worked well together, not least on the consultations. It would be worth examining the merits of establishing the NFER as an executive wing of NCC along with parts of the Assessment of Performance Unit, and the Further Education Unit, but this could only work if NCC achieved real independence.

(Graham with Tytler, 1993: 139)

This was not the first time that an influential partner had contemplated some sort of alliance with the Foundation (see the reference on page 50 to another such partnership arrangement that had been mooted with the Schools Council).

The winning of one of the SEAC contracts to develop standard assessment tasks for seven-year-olds was of major importance to the Foundation, although another bid to the same sponsor to develop assessment tasks for 14-year-olds was lost. These contracts would establish the Foundation in the forefront, both in this country and internationally, of the development of new assessment techniques. Another new sponsor this year was the Department of Health which commissioned the Foundation to conduct a major national evaluation of the new experimental approaches to general nurse education and training. This helped the Foundation to establish itself firmly in the area of professional training evaluation.

The NFER's two regional offices in Swansea and York were flourishing and were praised for promoting a positive image of the NFER in the areas they served. Both had attracted outside sponsorship. The track record of colleagues in Wales had enabled them to win two important SEAC contracts. In the Northern Office, Kay Kinder joined Dr John Harland: the pair of them were to play a pivotal role in developing the research programme and reputation of the office at York.

Another important new venture this year was the setting up of a separate commercial company, NFER Enterprises. The new company aimed to provide training in some of the salient new areas that had arisen from the implementation of the Education Reform Act, such as the local management of schools, as well as offering general consultancy services to LEAs and others. It was also intended that it should serve a wider audience than had hitherto been reached by the Foundation.

Professor WilliamTaylor, NFER Chairman 1983–1988

Collaboration with NFER-NELSON had been particularly fruitful with the successful launch of a number of new tests to meet the schools' emerging needs, including *Touchstones*, a new series of assessment tasks for children aged six to eight based on the principles put forward in the Task Group on Assessment and Testing (TGAT) report. Professor (later Sir) William Taylor had taken over the chairmanship in 1985 of the NFER-NELSON Publishing Company's Board of Directors, who were helping guide that company in their response to the rapidly changing demands of the market-place that had resulted from the far-reaching implications of the Education Reform Act.

While the NFER Presidency, occupied by Sir James Hamilton, had by now become a long-term appointment, Sir Wilfred Cockcroft had succeeded Professor William Taylor as Chairman of the Foundation's Board in December 1988. Sir Wilfred had been the Chairman and Chief Executive of the Secondary

Examinations Council. A new Foundation Honorary Treasurer was also appointed in the person of Mr Richard Bunker, the Director of Education for West Sussex, following four years of valuable service which had been given to the Foundation in this same role by Peter Edwards, Berkshire's Director of Education. A stalwart of past years, Leonard Brown, a former NFER Vice-President and Chairman of the Finance and General Purposes Committee from 1973 to 1983, was mourned for his loss. It was recorded that Professor Ben Morris had tendered his resignation from the Board on the date of the 40th anniversary of his appointment as Director of the NFER. Morris's place on the Board was taken by Lady Plowden, who chaired the committee which had produced the seminal report on primary education in 1967.

The Department of Assessment and Measurement was now at the cutting edge of the profound changes introduced in England and Wales as a result of the National Curriculum and the related assessments. A consortium, led by the NFER, which included Bishop Grosseteste College in Lincoln, the NFER-NELSON Publishing Company, and Sheffield and West Sussex LEAs, was one of three agencies awarded contracts to develop standard assessment tasks (SATs) for key stage 1 of the National Curriculum. The assessment tasks developed focused on the attainment targets in mathematics, science and English (or Welsh) and were cross-curricular in their nature, being derived from good primary practice. Beginning in January 1989, the work was scheduled for completion in August 1991 and also involved the development of in-service training for SATs and national assessment generally by the project team (Sainsbury, 1996).

The large samples required in the pilot testing for the development of SATs at key stages 1 and 3 also led to the setting up in 1989 of the School Coordinating Unit (SCU) at the NFER to coordinate the involvement of schools and LEAs on behalf of SEAC. The three similar services in the Foundation, the APU's Monitoring Services Unit, Field Research Services, and now the new SCU provided, through the Register of Schools, a means of contact with all the schools in England, Wales, and Northern Ireland which were involved in major research projects and were able thus to monitor the burden on those schools during this period of great change.

The Department of Information Research and Development had been commissioned by the National Audit Office to prepare a report on the LEAs' maintenance of school buildings, a survey of the immense task that would be needed to bring the stock of school building nationally up to an acceptable level.

BRIEF had developed *SIGNPOST*, an education guide specifically designed for the newly appointed advisers in the Department of Trade and Industry's Enterprise and Training Initiative.

The Department of Evaluation and Policy Studies work programme this year reflected the diverse range of topics and wider base of sponsors that were now being attracted by the Foundation. The Health Education Authority had commissioned the Foundation to evaluate a teaching pack and training programme on HIV/AIDS. Against a background which saw the advent of the Youth Training Scheme and the introduction of a unified system of National Vocational Qualifications, the Hairdressing Training Board sponsored the NFER to carry out a short research project to examine the effectiveness of trainee recruitment practices in the hairdressing industry. A more traditional survey, but one that none the less reflected the new provisions of the Education Reform Act 1988, was carried out into the aims and objectives of religious education in schools. Other projects researched that year included multicultural and antiracist policies; pastoral care and personal and social education issues; strategic quality management in the further education service; the impact of tertiary reorganisation and a heavy continuing involvement in the evaluation of TVEI.

In 1989, the Department of External Relations published the first issue of *TOPIC*, a new loose-leaf folio magazine developed with NFER-NELSON, whose articles were designed to appeal to classroom practitioners and to apply research conclusions to practice in current school situations. This Department also recorded the increasing interest by the news media in the work of the Foundation and its outcomes. The courses and conferences programme continued to expand, meeting the much increased need for in-service training (INSET) and development courses as both schools and the LEAs geared themselves to adapt to the avalanche of new legislative requirements.

The Department of Professional Studies' work programme included projects on the education of children in care; parental involvement in children's schooling; the recruitment, retention and motivation of headteachers and deputy heads; teacher stress, and the evaluation of nurse education and training.

Internally, a system of formal departmental reviews had been implemented. An Equal Opportunities Policy for the Foundation had also been adopted and pilot testing of a staff appraisal scheme had begun. Yet another attempt was being made at a standardised image with the announcement that a new logo and uniform house style was being adopted for the Foundation's output. Work began to erect a new building at the Foundation's headquarters, with consequent noise and disruption during what proved to be a long, hot summer. As a part of this programme of work, a demountable building was at last removed from what had been the Bentleys' croquet lawn. By the time the 44th Annual Report for 1989–90 was published, the new accommodation – which was named the Bentley Building, to commemorate the family who built The Mere – had been officially opened in June 1990 by Mrs Angela Rumbold, then the Minister of State for Education, and herself an ex-member of the Foundation's Board of Management.

Opening of the Bentley Building, June 1990.

Dr Clare Burstall, Angela Rumbold MP and Rosalind Bentley

There was now considerable activity on the international front. The NFER was part of a developing consortium of European educational research institutions and, in June 1989, hosted a working meeting of the group. The Director was invited to speak about the Foundation's work (which had now put it at the leading edge of assessment development), in Australia, Canada and the USA. Dr Burstall was also invited to address the Council of Local Education Authorities at their annual conference in Bradford on the same theme. Nearly 7,000 pupils from 18 LEAs had been involved in the SATs pilot and, on the basis of these trials, the Foundation's report to SEAC had advocated a much-reduced future assessment framework.

David Streatfield took up the new post of Managing Director of NFER Enterprises Ltd, with his core team, also recruited internally from existing staff members, working from their new base in The Mere. Dr Burstall wrote that: 'If energy, enthusiasm and commitment are anything to go by, they deserve to do very well indeed.' Dick Bunker, the Foundation's Honorary Treasurer, also took on the Chairmanship of the new NFER Enterprises Board of Directors.

This year the Foundation was subject to review by the Central Bodies Advisory Group (CBAG) in respect of the grant it received from the local authorities under what was by now Section 78(1) of the Local Government Finance Act, 1988. The CBAG assessors commented positively on the work and management efficiency of the Foundation as a result of their scrutiny. Sponsored income had again reached an all-time high.

Two of those long associated with leading the Foundation died that year: Sir Alan Lubbock, a Vice-President, and a former Director, Professor Ben Morris. Mrs Nicole Harrison now took on the acting chairmanship of the Board from Sir Wilfrid Cockcroft.

The 45th Annual Report for 1990–91 announced that Miss Joyce Baird OBE, formerly the Joint General Secretary of the Assistant Masters and Mistresses Association, had become the first woman Vice-President of the Foundation in December 1990. Lord Peston, Emeritus Professor of Economics at Queen Mary College, London, and who had once been a Special Adviser to the Secretary of State for Education, became the Chairman of the Board of Management at the same time.

In accordance with the CBAG recommendations of the previous year, the research undertaken as part of the Membership Programme was now agreed after joint discussions with representatives of the Local Authority Associations. Another of the CBAG recommendations was that the Foundation should expand its desktop publishing activities in order to disseminate its research findings more widely. The acquisition of better desktop equipment and staff training helped to achieve this objective and the year witnessed an unprecedented increase in the production of research reports and training materials.

Chapter 8

Testing Times
1990–1993

The Foundation's testing and assessment work had often been seen as controversial in the past. Now, its involvement in the introduction of the National Curriculum had placed the NFER even more under the bright glare of media attention. Dr Burstall, who had served on the Secretary of State's Task Group on Assessment and Testing (TGAT),[1] wrote of the Foundation hitting the headlines when the NFER-led consortium won the contract to develop the standard assessment tasks (SATs) for key stage 1 in both English and Welsh, and at key stage 3 in Welsh. Projects investigating reading standards, the value of different methods of teaching reading, and of preparing trainee teachers for the task of teaching beginners to read, had also attracted a great deal of publicity, being work that had '…contributed a welcome objectivity to a public debate which has sometimes been conducted more on the basis of anecdote than of evidence'.

The Director also wrote of the increasing difficulties faced by the Foundation's staff, even following the hard task of winning a research contract: 'It is not unknown for sponsors to move the goalposts while the match is still in play. Project teams are then left to cope with the effects on tight timetables and fixed budgets of delayed or reversed decisions, major policy changes, unexpected demands, suddenly advanced deadlines, and so on. They do cope, but at some cost to themselves: leave is postponed, long hours become the norm.' This was a far more demanding and politicised environment in which the Foundation now found itself striving to perform its role and maintain its integrity.

Internally, a statement of corporate aims for the Foundation and a code of good practice were being prepared. Dr Judy Bradley was instrumental in writing a comprehensive staff development policy, which was implemented to complement the staff appraisal scheme then being piloted.

A Research Seminar Group, composed of individuals nominated from the Foundation's various departments, had organised a series of talks delivered in the staff lunch hour, an annual programme involving both external and internal speakers. This Group realised that those working at the greatly expanded NFER in ever more pressurised and specialised roles were becoming increasingly isolated from each other. This led them to organise, in the summer of 1990, the first Staff Conference Day, one day that was to be set aside from normal routines so all staff could choose from a varied series of presentations by colleagues about their work and research methods, followed by the enjoyment of some more relaxed social and sporting activities later in the day.

As was now the pattern, a new record income of £4,383,000 was recorded, being a 9.5 per cent increase on the previous year: nearly two-thirds of this was earned by external funding, sponsored research having increased by 13 per cent.

A Staff Conference Day. Staff gathered before The Mere's south frontage

£914,000 came from the Local Authority Associations for the Membership Programme and was used to fund research into the implications for LEAs of the implementation of the Education Reform Act from the curriculum management standpoint; the impact of LMS on the changing role of LEAs; school governance issues, etc., as well as for the services of EMIE, the Library and Information Services, and other Foundation support services.

NFER-NELSON contributed £389,000 in royalties and profits to the Foundation. The other partner in this Company, Thomas Nelson and Sons Ltd, owned by the Thomson Corporation, transferred its share during the year to Routledge, another subsidiary of the International Thomson Group, which acquired the company's books and journals list.

However, it was reported that

One unhappy episode marred the run of this year's successes. In spite of the valiant efforts of all members of staff, NFER Enterprises, which we launched last year as a subsidiary company, never really got off the ground. We were forced early this year to put the company into liquidation, with consequent distress to all concerned. With hindsight, the idea was good but the timing was not. In a period of recession, training activities are one of the first to be curtailed: it is now clear that NFER Enterprises was trying to establish itself as a training agency at the least propitious moment.

(NFER Annual Report, 1990–91)

Its demise involved both a significant financial loss and the departure of all of its staff, who had, individually, given the Foundation both long and loyal service.

The Director commented again in the 46th Annual Report for 1991–92 on the 'cut-throat competition, shorter deadlines, tighter funding, and the need to respond swiftly and positively to a succession of policy changes affecting our research programme'. Dr Burstall wrote that the Foundation's work had attracted 'a great deal of media attention, most of it positive, although we have learned to live with the fact that those who raise their heads above the parapet must expect the occasional sniper!' The organisation now had to be increasingly active in promoting itself in an era of changing demands. As Stuart Maclure observed in an interview with Nick Tester, this was the period when the

Foundation became entrepreneurial in its activities. The NFER's expertise was now much in demand abroad, and many requests for help and advice were received from the newly democratised countries of central and eastern Europe, 'most of whom are setting up national research institutions from scratch and desperately need training in managerial skills'. The Foundation had often been asked to provide advice and practical help also to research agencies such as the Organisation for Economic Co-operation and Development (OECD), the Council of Europe, the World Bank, and the British Council. Additionally, the NFER had hosted visiting researchers and continued to play an active role in international projects of a collaborative nature.

During this period, the Foundation continued to enhance its well-deserved reputation for work in psychometrics and test development. Chris Whetton, the Head of the Department of Assessment and Measurement, also wrote in the Annual Report about the keen attention that the media had given to testing and assessment during the year. The production of standard tasks for SEAC at key stage 1 continued and they were used by 30,000 teachers in 1992 to test half a million children. Assessments for history were being developed at the same stage. Work on the National Curriculum assessment at key stage 3 in mathematics, science, English and technology was also being undertaken by the NFER in association with Brunel University. Test development had not been confined to the school years: a literacy test for the Office of Population Censuses and Surveys had been produced for possible use in the 1993 General Household Survey. In the area of occupational tests, a series of Critical Reasoning Tests had been produced for the selection of junior managers.

In the Department of Professional Studies, some projects had had to change tack during their course in order to respond to new developments in the management and financing of education. A project on *Active Life for Handicapped Youth: Integration in the School*, which was funded by the OECD/CERI, enabled the Foundation to work jointly with fellow professionals in the Scottish Council for Research in Education and the Northern Ireland Council for Educational Research. The Department's work in the Health Service received another boost with a new contract from the Department of Health for a study of nurse education in the area of HIV/AIDS.

The Department of Evaluation and Policy Studies had sought to widen its sponsorship base yet further and to apply its research skills to new domains. An interesting spread of sponsors included: the Construction Industry Training Board, English Nature, the National Westminster Bank, the Gaelic Medium College of Further Education, and the European Commission. The Department was making more use of a technique known as 'multi-level modelling' as an evaluation tool; it had also expanded the use of telephone interviewing methods as a speedy, cost-efficient means of gathering data from practitioners.

The Department of Curriculum Studies had been much concerned with the perennially topical area of standards in education. It was conducting projects on changes in reading performance over an interval of time and the teaching of reading in schools, as well as an international study of mathematics and science in 20 countries. Although the main work of the Assessment of Performance Unit had ceased some years ago, several of this Department's staff were former members of the APU teams. The Evaluation and Monitoring Unit of the School Examinations and Assessment Council (SEAC), which had taken over the APU's remaining affairs, had sponsored the establishment of an archive of APU data and materials for three subjects which the NFER teams were commissioned to survey, *viz.* mathematics, languages and modern foreign languages. The APU data was now being used on a SEAC-sponsored project studying the differential performance of boys and girls in GCSE English and Mathematics (Foxman *et al.*, 1991).

In the Department of Information and External Services, EMIE continued to provide a range of overviews that were indicative of current concerns in the LEAs. The original focus of the EURYDICE Network, of which EPIC Europe (as it was now called at the Foundation) was a part, had been to provide a formal, written question and answer service. The unit at the NFER, which was led by Joanna Le Métais, served the policy makers in the LEAs in England and Wales, and Northern Ireland's Education and Library Boards, as well as the increasing number of government-funded agencies. From the early 1990s, the EURYDICE Network began the publication of standardised Europe-wide information documents on education systems and policies. EPIC Europe was now responsible for producing a National Dossier describing the education system in England and Wales for the benefit of others in the European Community. This National Dossier was subsequently incorporated into the EURYDICE Network's database on education systems – EURYBASE. More detailed thematic studies were also produced such as *The Teaching of Modern Foreign Languages in Primary and Secondary Education in the European Community* in 1992. The

Network also began in the mid-1990s to produce European comparative studies such as *Measures to Combat Failure at Schools: A Challenge for the Construction of Europe* (1994).

The Foundation's efforts to produce rapid and wide spread dissemination of research findings were greatly enhanced by the development of an in-house book production system and the skilled use of modern technology, with over 30 books or pamphlets now produced to a high standard of design. A new monthly periodical, *Education News Digest*, was launched in conjunction with *The Times Educational Supplement*. Field Research Services and the School Coordinating Unit had contacted over 16,000 schools in connection with the NFER's research programmes involving evaluations and questionnaire surveys and test development work – an increase of more than 50 per cent on the schools contacted in the previous year.

A breakdown of the Foundation's income in the Annual Report for the year ending 31 March 1992 showed that 59 per cent of income came from sponsored research, with a nine per cent increase this year to over £3 million. The Local Authority Associations' grant this year was £981,000. Despite having had a difficult year, the NFER-NELSON Publishing Company still managed to contribute £502,000 to the Foundation as its half share of the annual profits, together with royalties of £131,000, which amounted to 13 per cent of the Foundation's income. This figure of £633,000 had, however, included a sum of £214,000 from the sale of the Book Division to Routledge.

For the second year, a Staff Conference Day was set aside in June during which staff were able to present aspects of their work to colleagues, an occasion that helped understanding and communication between those working in Slough and their colleagues from the regional offices at Swansea and York, who were also present. Held in the high summer season, these Staff Conference Days were continued in the years that followed and offered a unique annual opportunity for all Foundation staff to meet together at The Mere, and on its sunlit lawns. These occasions have also included photographic competitions, and arts and crafts displays, which revealed a range of extramural talents present among the NFER's employees.

The fine grounds surrounding The Mere proved not only a boon to occasions such as Staff Conference Days but have also provided the opportunity for the more energetic of the staff to exercise their limbs and demonstrate their sporting prowess. Cricket, croquet, netball, rounders, and table tennis have all been played by NFER staff on the Bentleys' lawns – which were used for some of these activities during the family's own occupation – while nearby badminton, squash and tennis courts have provided the opportunity for others to challenge their colleagues. (The purchase of croquet balls for use in games played by some of the staff on The Mere's lawns, as recorded in the NFER Social Club's accounts in the 1980s, might be viewed as a reflection of a somewhat less harried era in the life of the Foundation.) Together with a five-a-side indoor soccer team, the NFER has also run its own cricket team, started in 1982, which brought some sporting silverware to The Mere. Playing in a league composed of other laboratory and research institutions in the Thames Valley, the Foundation's cricket team – led by Keith Mason, who demonstrated over 16 seasons exceptional skill as both a player and an inspiring team captain – clinched the league championship title in the summer of 1991. Another of the

NFER's Cricket Team celebrates its 1991 League Championship victory

founders of the cricket XI, Robert Butler, became its most prolific run-scoring batsman in the 18 years he played for the club, setting records that are unlikely to be surpassed. The NFER's cricket team, true to the Foundation's inclusive and egalitarian principles, has in its time included a number of women cricketers (one of these, Wendy Fader, was a player of county-capped standard) as well as those of more mature years and mixed sporting abilities.

From the 1970s, regular Christmas shows, some of them cast in the guise of traditional pantomimes, were performed at The Mere. These too provided opportunities for staff to demonstrate perhaps hitherto unsuspected talents, both on stage and in supporting roles, to their colleagues. Foremost among those with acting and directing talents on the staff were Mavis Froud and Kim Halliday. General knowledge quizzes organised by Neil Hagues (a long-time stalwart of the NFER Social Club committee in its time) also became popular in the 1990s, providing both intellectual stimulus and continuing the honourable tradition of fund-raising by the staff for a variety of charities in the process. These out-of-

office staff social activities served to bring together an increasingly mobile and much-expanded work force whose compartmentalised roles might otherwise have provided little opportunity for them to mix with Foundation colleagues.

At the end of the 1960s, a House Committee, consisting of representatives of the staff and management, had been formed in order to deal with issues of practical concern at The Mere. One subject that repeatedly occupied the Committee's attention was the contentious issue of smoking by staff within the Foundation's premises. The interests of the NFER's employees were also looked after for many years by its own Staff Association, in which Margaret Reid played a prominent position. The Association of Clerical, Technical and Supervisory Staff trade union later took on the representation of the interests of its members, and of the staff in general, at the Foundation. Dr Greg Brooks – who became one of the country's foremost literacy researchers at the NFER – acted for many years as a representative of the union in its negotiations with the Foundation's management.

The Heads of Department provided detailed accounts of the work of their colleagues in the 47th Annual Report for 1992–93. Chris Whetton, Head of the Department of Assessment and Measurement, wrote that 'the last 12 months have proved to be as busy and challenging as any year which has gone before. Work continued on various tasks concerned with assessment at key stages 1, 2 and 3... the Department remains at the centre of developments of assessments in Britain, both in traditional psychometric areas and in National Curriculum assessment'.

The Department of Professional Studies' sponsors this year included the Arts Council, the Baring Foundation, and the Alcohol Education and Research Council. Work on the financial management of education expanded and a number of projects were undertaken in this area. The Department's portfolio of research in the arts received a significant boost with *Youth Participation in the Arts*, carried out by staff in the Northern Office who proceeded to build up a particular expertise in the area of arts education. The Health Service remained an important focus of their research activities and the *National Evaluation of Demonstration Schemes in Pre-registration Nurse Education (Project 2000)* was completed this year.

Dr Sheila Stoney, Head of Evaluation and Policy Studies, also reported her Department having had its busiest ever year, with a widened sponsorship base.

Three new projects had been added to their portfolio of Employment Department research: the continuing evaluation of Training Credits; the evaluation of the Compacts extension; and the development of tools to measure the learning outcomes of guidance. 'Compacts' were an initiative that involved school–business partnerships in the inner cities. The Foundation's evaluation of the Compacts was one of the first projects to utilise a 'value-added' approach, involving measuring the progress of cohorts of young people against national performance indicators. As was the case with the LAPP and TVEI initiatives, the expertise gained on the Compacts evaluation led to a succession of other research commissions being won by the NFER.

A major study of multicultural education had been completed by Monica Taylor, and review and development projects in both values and environmental education were under way. This Department's own involvement in health issues too continued with a national study of health education policies. It also had a growing number of projects which had attracted European funding.

Dr Derek Foxman, Head of the Department of Curriculum Studies, reported on the work that had been conducted for England's participation in the Third International Mathematics and Science Study (TIMSS). The Foundation had now also been commissioned by SEAC to carry out an analysis of the Review of The National Curriculum and Assessment Framework by Sir Ron Dearing (Barber, 1996:62–5).

Press interest in the Foundation and its research outcomes continued with several authors of NFER reports having conducted 'on-air' interviews, thereby reaching an ever-wider audience with the outcomes of their research and boosting the public's knowledge of the organisation.

As part of its strong commitment to improve the conditions of service for Foundation staff and to enhance the effectiveness of its activities, a landmark change in the NFER's employment practice took place in 1993. The NFER moved from a situation where most research staff were employed on short-term contracts to one where all staff who had satisfactorily completed their probation were given open-ended contracts. This far-sighted change enabled the Foundation to provide more flexibility in staffing projects and to further the opportunities for staff to extend their research experience and skills. The move towards enhanced staff security also served the NFER well in recruiting and retaining high-quality staff. No longer would an ever-present threat of redundancy at the end of a project be a part of the life-style of the NFER's research staff.

Although income, at £4,805,000, was down from last year's record level, this was because the previous year had contained a windfall with the sale of the books and publications list to Routledge. The Local Authority Associations' grant topped the £1million mark for the first time this year with a figure of £1,045,000 being given to the Foundation. NFER-NELSON had a record-breaking year with £446,000 being paid to the Foundation from its earned income (just under ten per cent of the total income). 7.5 per cent of the Foundation's other income (£363,000) was earned this year by the sales of its Computing and Statistical Services, and of its own publications.

Dr Burstall announced her retirement after 30 years of working for the Foundation in the 47th Annual Report. Her many years of devoted service had spanned the Foundation's substantial growth from its Wimpole Street days, when the NFER had been best known for its work on secondary school selection and comprehensive reorganisation, to a time when the Foundation found itself thrust even more centre stage through the much increased involvement of politicians in curriculum and assessment issues. As well as its enormously raised national profile, the NFER's success in winning contracts in these areas of development had gained it much international attention. Dr Burstall had been keenly alert to the new players and pressures that would henceforth shape the field of education and had skilfully ensured in her time as Director that the Foundation would continue to capitalise on its wide expertise.

Note

[1] 'Essentially, TGAT attempted to produce a system which would have credibility among sceptical professionals, while simultaneously meeting the government's political demand for accountability. In the end, this circle proved impossible to square' (Barber,1996:53).

Chapter 9

Golden Jubilee
1994–1996

After a period as Acting Director, Dr Seamus
Hegarty was appointed to lead the Foundation in
June 1994. Seamus Hegarty was raised in Cork and
had entered a seminary in Ireland for six years.
Opting afterwards to teach, which he did in both
Dublin and London, he also took a doctorate in
communications studies in the University of
London. Following a period with a management
training company, Seamus Hegarty joined the
NFER in 1975 where he built up a reputation, both
in this country and internationally, for the research
he undertook into special educational needs. In
1983, Dr Hegarty was made the Foundation's
Deputy Director. After his appointment as Director,
a new senior management team structure was put in
place; the post of Deputy Director disappeared and the five heads of department
were then replaced with four posts designated as Assistant Directors.

Dr Seamus Hegarty,
Director
1993–present

In his first Annual Report, for 1993–94, Dr Hegarty wrote of the departure of
three senior colleagues who between them had devoted 65 years of service to the
Foundation – Barbara Bloomfield, who had been awarded the MBE in the 1985
New Year Honours List for her work leading the NFER's Field Research
Services and the SEAC School Coordinating Unit, and another two staff
members who had been Heads of Department, Dr Derek Foxman and Dr Ray
Sumner. Ralph Tabberer was welcomed on his return to the NFER's staff,
joining the team of Assistant Directors.

The new Director commented on the now highly politicised nature of education which provided further challenges to the research enterprise and how 'A national education and training system that aspires towards ever higher standards has need of research to clarify policy options, assist in implementing them and evaluate their impact on practice.'

The Foundation's research activity encompassed 116 projects over that year – 73 of them new project starts – and generated a turnover of nearly £5 million. As well as ongoing work in the field of National Curriculum assessment for the School Curriculum and Assessment Authority (SCAA), and numerous major evaluation projects for the Employment Department, these projects spanned some of the principal educational concerns of the day. In order to disseminate the outcomes of this wide-ranging research, 23 reports were published in-house and more by individual sponsors. Particular attention was paid to improving media coverage of NFER reports, which proved so successful that it was reported that 'Few weeks now pass without some reference to our work in the main educational press.'

The Department of Assessment and Measurement experienced a year of growth and diversification. Work continued on National Curriculum assessment in key stages 1, 2 and 3. They also continued to provide consultancy advice to organisations as diverse as the LEAs, the Adult Literacy and Basic Skills Unit, the Business and Technology Education Council, the Transport Research Laboratory, the Home Office and an insurance company. An exciting new venture for this Department was its involvement in the development of the new theory test for learner drivers and riders that was introduced in 1996. It was a project that proved to be extremely innovative both in applying technology and in the trialling of representative samples of candidates, which included some among the Foundation's own staff. The Department's success in winning this project, and a large number of other assessment contracts, illustrated the Foundation's continuing high reputation in applied assessment development across a wide variety of contexts and subject matter.

A new Department of Professional and Curriculum Studies arose from the merger of the formerly separate Departments of Professional Studies and Curriculum Studies in January 1994, with Dr Judy Bradley as its new Head. Research on literacy had long been one of the Foundation's major areas of interest and this year the Department investigated reading standards in Northern

Ireland, and trends in the reading attainment of eight-year-olds, as well as evaluating the Adult Literacy and Basic Skills Unit's Family Literacy Programme. The Department's programme of research in the field of the arts and the media continued to flourish with a Department of National Heritage-sponsored project into the role of attitudes in influencing levels of participation in the arts, heritage and sports. Dr Bradley's new Department also took on responsibility for the Northern Office, which continued to flourish with the strong support given by the Foundation's senior management.

The Department of Evaluation and Policy Studies under Dr Sheila Stoney had undertaken a series of short, and often complex, projects. A significant research development was the contract won from the Health Education Authority to evaluate the impact of the European Network of Health Promoting Schools in England. This Department had become responsible for the NFER's Welsh Office, which, building on its success as a leader in the development of national assessments tests and support material in the Welsh language, was now taking on the Welsh end of various national projects as well as developing its own portfolio of research and evaluation for sponsors in Wales.

Restructuring also took place to bring all the Foundation's information-based services and projects together in a new Information Department, headed by Ralph Tabberer. A research and consultancy programme was also developed by attracting funding for critical reviews and the evaluation of research in specific areas, and through research into the use of new technologies in education.

The Statistics Service was now becoming increasingly involved in the school effectiveness (value added) area and was carrying out work on behalf of local education authorities.

Overall income at £4,994,00 was 3.9 per cent up on the previous year with the Local Authority Associations' grant at £1,073,000. The NFER-NELSON Publishing Company had another record-breaking year with a figure of £492,000 being received by the Foundation. Income from a number of other sources, including investments and the sale of computer time, Statistical Services' expertise and in-house publishing, also yielded £401,000 which was used for the Foundation's Additional Activities Programme. A graph in the 48th Annual Report illustrated the growth of the Foundation's income over the previous 20 years from £453,000 to over ten times that figure in 1993–94.

In the 49th Annual Report for 1994–95, Dr Hegarty presented an insightful overview of developments:

The painstaking amassing and analysis of evidence and the insistence on affirming only what is supported by evidence are not activities which commend themselves to everybody. It is necessary to make the case for them continually. If the primacy of evidence and reasoned argument is not acknowledged, policy making is prey to sectional interests and partial perspectives and practice will fail to benefit from analysed experience. While we have to accept that research is – quite properly – only one input to policy making, it is an essential one. Research can clarify policy options, assist in implementation and evaluate outcomes. More broadly, research gives a better understanding of what is going on in the education system and in that way helps to improve the provision of education and training. The challenge to the research community is to ensure that its voice is heard. Too often in the past perhaps we have been content to let our findings speak for themselves. That is no longer an appropriate stance, if indeed it ever was. We have to ensure that we present our research findings clearly and that we communicate effectively with our different audiences.

(NFER Annual Report, 1994–5)

Particular attention was being paid to dissemination of the Foundation's research output: 26 new reports were published in-house, in addition to the numerous articles and papers written by staff. The scale of the dissemination task was illustrated by the fact that researchers had worked on a total of 112 projects in the course of the year with 63 coming to an end. The Foundation continued to raise its profile through media coverage of its reports and engaging in the educational debate of issues. Local government reorganisation had formed an important backdrop to the NFER's work that year and the EMIE service faced growing demands for information with the emergence of a considerable number of smaller education authorities. Sponsored research income had grown by more than 40 per cent, an unprecedented increase. This had necessitated taking on new staff and making substantial investment in information technology. It also led to severe pressure on space and discussions were started on how to secure additional accommodation.

A high level of investment was being made in staff development by the Foundation and a formal commitment had been given to secure 'Investors in People' status. As another tangible indication of this resolve, nine members of the support staff gained an NVQ Level 2 in Business Administration in the course of the year.

In April 1995, David May-Bowles retired after serving the Foundation since 1967, the last six of those years as Company Secretary and Head of Finance. Adrian Clark joined the Foundation as his replacement in these roles.

The scope and range of the Department of Assessment and Measurement's projects continued to expand, encompassing tests for every age from two to 65, while including subjects as diverse as hearing vocabulary and hazard perception in drivers. Their research projects fell into three areas: those for tests intended for publication; National Curriculum tests and tasks; and specialised development for particular purposes. The NFER continued to be the leading institution involved in the development of end-of-key stage tests. The major project in the area of specialised development was the theory test for drivers and riders, which became compulsory in July 1996. As well as the written test of knowledge and understanding of driving theory and practice, a secondary part of the project involved the development of a computerised test to assess skill in the detection of potential hazard situations. The diversity of this Department's projects was testimony to the range of expertise of its staff in many curriculum areas: in psychological assessment; in psychometrics and educational measurement; and in complex production and development procedures.

A great deal of media attention was generated by a project undertaken by the Department of Professional and Curriculum Studies which looked at strategies for addressing the 'summer-born effect' on children's educational attainment: the report by Caroline Sharp on this study sold in high numbers.

Two long-term evaluation projects in the Department of Evaluation and Policy Studies were concluded this year, *viz.* the *National Evaluation of Urban Compacts* and the *Cohort Study of TVEI Extension Students*. A major study on the role of the Careers Service in schools was also completed. A project on environmental education had also been under way for two years.

The NFER's value added service to schools, known as QUASE (Quantitative Analysis for Self-Evaluation), was formally launched in 1994 to provide a rigorous analysis of a school's, and individual departments', performance at GCSE, taking account of pupil ability and other contextual factors. Also begun in 1994 was the first of what became a series of NFER Annual Surveys of Trends in Education. These consisted of questionnaire surveys of primary school headteachers which were intended to collect and then disseminate up-to-date views on current issues in education.

The Library and Information Services Staff, 1996

The Information Department had now united a number of services at the Foundation whose specialised information management skills gave access to, and use of, information about past and current research in education; LEA educational policies and programmes; and about educational systems in the UK and other European countries. Following the signing of the Treaty of Maastricht, which brought the field of education within the sphere of the European Community, EURYDICE became part of SOCRATES, the official Community education programme. In 1995, EPIC Europe won a five-year contract from the DfEE to continue to provide the national EURYDICE Unit under the first phase of the SOCRATES programme. The Library continued to undertake an annual survey of current educational research in the United Kingdom for the *Register of Educational Research in the United Kingdom*, which was now published by Routledge.

The School Coordinating Unit undertook an exercise on behalf of the SCAA whereby 1.3 million pupil names from schools in England and Wales, involved in the assessment at key stages 2 and 3, were collected and printed on marksheets to facilitate the marking and collation of results.

Overall income was up by 28 per cent to £6,397,000, with sponsored research at £4,295,000 accounting for 67 per cent of the total, which was again a new record for the Foundation. The Local Authority Associations' grant was increased by 3.4 per cent to £1,110,000. The Additional Activities Programme benefited from a 21 per cent increase in income from NFER-NELSON with a £438,000 share of the profits as well as a 12 per cent increase in royalties (£148,000) this year.

In the Foundation's 50th Annual Report for 1995–96, the Director wrote a considered Introduction on the current state of research activity in the NFER's

'Golden Jubilee' year.

The organisation of educational research gained a good deal of attention during the year. Two reviews, under Leverhulme and ESRC auspices respectively, were completed, and the British Educational Research Association initiated a debate on the role of educational research. Within the university sector, where staff have long aspired to combine teaching and researching, the current Research Assessment Exercise places a premium on research activities. Teachers too are being encouraged by the Teacher Training Agency and others to regard teaching as a research-based profession and to carry out their own research whenever possible. Such attention is to be welcomed, particularly if it expands the national research capacity. The conduct of research is not the exclusive preserve of full-time, professional researchers and additions to the body of research findings must be welcomed wherever they come from.

(NFER Annual Report, 1995–96)

He felt that it was naïve to think that the conflating of teaching and researching was conducive to excellence in either, however. 'The conduct of research on a sustained basis is facilitated by the presence of certain conditions: a body of skilled staff dedicated to research; links with the relevant academic, policy and practice contexts; a dissemination ethos backed by adequate resources; and a support infrastructure that provides a full range of underpinning services.' These conditions could not be met either in the university or school teaching contexts, he felt. 'All of this means a key role for dedicated research institutions such as the NFER.'

Assessment continued as a major area of the Foundation's work. Dr Hegarty observed in the Foundation's own journal that: 'The processes of test development are specialised… These activities require considerable organisational and professional expertise, and the Foundation has the largest group of people with this expertise working in one organisation in Britain…[Its] current level of activity reflects the continuous tradition of the 50 years of assessment research and test development' (Hegarty, 1996:248–9).

The NFER remained a leading institution in the development of tests for National Curriculum assessment, with projects covering pupils aged 7–14 and spanning English, mathematics and science. Close collaboration between the Foundation and the NFER-NELSON Publishing Company made a significant contribution to the latter's commercial success and provided a wide range of assessment materials for diverse use. The Foundation had also been working on the Customised Testing project, a pioneering development in the generation and distribution of item bank tests, covering mathematics, English, verbal reasoning, and non-verbal reasoning. This work had opened up exciting possibilities for the precise specification of tests and for their delivery in an electronic mode. In a completely different sphere, work on the theory test for drivers had led to what has possibly been the Foundation's best seller ever, i.e. *The Complete Theory Test for Cars and Motorcycles*.

A member of the Evaluation and Policy Studies Department was working with a cross-national group of teachers and researchers, under the auspices of the Consortium of Institutions for Development and Research in Education in Europe, to develop effective cross-national approaches to school self-evaluation. (The Foundation had been a prime mover in CIDREE's establishment, another example of the strong international links it sought to forge.) For over ten years, staff in the Department had been national evaluators of TVEI, the major 14–18 initiative of that period, and it was continuing to build upon that tradition. The Department was also seeking to extend its project base from the school-to-work area, in which it already had a significant presence, to mainstream training issues and had gained three commissions from the DfEE in the area of vocational qualifications.

A further 28 titles had now been added to NFER's catalogue of published reports and the journal *TOPIC* entered its sixth year of publication with an increased subscription base. A welcome development over the year was the growing strength of the two regional offices. The Welsh Office in Swansea, established in 1978 to develop Welsh language assessments, had conducted a steady stream of work on assessment issues since that time. Its expanding numbers of staff had successively occupied three premises in Swansea, being based first with the Department of Education at the University College, then occupying a converted house, and subsequently moving to a modern, purpose-built office block in an enterprise zone on the outskirts of the city. Following a deliberate strategy to broaden the Welsh Office's terms of reference and base of expertise, it had begun conducting research and evaluation activities in addition to test and assessment development. The Northern Office in York, set up in 1986 as a result of the work on LAPP undertaken in Sheffield Polytechnic, had a particular concern with the research and intelligence needs of the schools and LEAs in the north of England as well as carrying out national projects. Its expanding team of researchers had established a reputation particularly for work on arts education; teachers' continuing professional development; and pupil disaffection. The Director commented that the work of these offices was not only important in its own right but that they also played a significant role 'in ensuring that the Foundation remains truly national and is not unduly focused on the metropolitan concerns of London and the South East'.

The Foundation's national role did not preclude a significant international involvement, and the Director cited the work of the Education Policy Information Centre, Europe, as well as the growing portfolio of projects with a specifically international dimension. The NFER continued to take an active leadership role in networks such as the Consortium of Institutions for Development and Research in Education in Europe, the European Union Network for Assessment, Effectiveness and Innovation, and the European Educational Research Association. During its special Golden Jubilee year, the Foundation also acted as host to the General Assembly of the Assessment, Effectiveness and Innovation Network at Slough.

Accommodation, for so long a regular item in the Foundation's Annual Reports, was once again a preoccupation. The growth seen in recent years had by now placed a considerable pressure on the accommodation, and a warning was given that 'all the facilities at The Mere are fully used, whether accommodation, computer facilities, furniture, telephone lines, meeting rooms or just storage space. With utilisation at 100 per cent, additional facilities will have to be acquired to accommodate any further research expansion.' A feasibility study had indicated that a new building was seen as a necessity and a formal application to develop the site at The Mere was shortly to be submitted.

The year saw a further increase in turnover of 11 per cent to £6,993,000. Sponsored research accounted for 64 per cent of the income (£4,419,000), an increase of six per cent over the previous year. During the year, work was undertaken on a total of 127 different sponsored projects from 61 different sponsors, continuing the upward trend and reflecting the success of efforts to win new sponsors. However, the Membership Programme grant from the local authorities was held on a standstill basis, with grant increased by less than one per cent to £1,119,000, against which expenditure rose by 6.75 per cent.

While the Annual Reports often record the achievements of named research staff, no less valuable members of the family of workers at the NFER are those in support roles, such as its catering staff – the Foundation having been well served by a succession of those who had ministered over the years to the 'inner man and woman' in its staff canteen – and those who performed a range of vital duties about its buildings and grounds. Joe Sharp, the Building and Grounds Officer who retired in 1995 after 15 years with the NFER, continued the tradition – like Bob Bannister (1964–1975) before him – of giving meticulous care to the

fine grounds which surround The Mere. Their long and devoted service is representative of generations of employees who have performed a wide variety of tasks to ensure the smooth and orderly functioning of a community of people at the Foundation.

The Mere and its grounds in winter

In the Golden Jubilee Annual Report, Dr Hegarty looked back on the Foundation's first 50 years as a period which spanned enormous socio-cultural and technological, as well as educational, changes. The NFER's success was, he felt, a remarkable story not only of achievement in the face of pervasive doubts on the value of research but also of the vision of those many people committed to creating a national research capacity which would support educational improvements. To celebrate this special anniversary, a number of national and international events were organised by the Foundation including a residential conference to examine the current situation of educational research and its role, and to consider how it could best inform policy and practice at a national level. Many of the leading researchers from Britain and around the world came together at a venue in Windsor in December 1996 to take stock of these issues: the later publication of its proceedings provided an important overview of opinions on the role that is played internationally by educational research (Hegarty, 1997). The list of participants in this conference was a reflection of the esteem in which the Foundation is held both in this country and abroad, and of how greatly it had developed since its establishment. The Director was well aware, however, that in celebrating the NFER's Golden Jubilee the Foundation had also to address itself to future challenges as:

> the changes we have seen over the past 50 years are as nothing in comparison with the changes we shall see over the next 50.

> (Hegarty, 1997:14)

Epilogue
1996 and beyond

By the time it reached its 50th anniversary, the Foundation had established itself as a highly respected part of the educational and research community, being one of the largest independent bodies of its kind in Britain, or elsewhere in the world. Throughout this half century the Foundation had demonstrated an ability to contribute its research expertise to the evolving issues of the time, be it the 11-plus and secondary selection; the move towards comprehensive education; or the introduction of monitoring and National Curriculum assessment. The NFER's assessment and measurement activities, which had traditionally formed the core of its work, had continued to flourish and diversify, gaining a variety of important contracts. The Foundation's reputation and enterprise had gained it major and long-running contracts for national evaluations such as those for the Assessment of Performance Unit, the Lower Attaining Pupils Programme and the Technical and Vocational Education Initiative. At a time when the role of teachers became increasingly complex and challenging, the NFER had supported their professional development. It undertook research and evaluation on initial and in-service teacher training, staff development and appraisal, producing resource packs and open-learning materials. In turn, this had also led on to the Foundation providing support and training for related professional groups.

The NFER steadily enlarged the scope of its research activities to cover a wide number of areas. As further education had progressed from local technical colleges to become a major player in post-16 education, an initial contract awarded in the 1960s to study day and block release courses gradually grew into a comprehensive portfolio of projects. Following moves towards more integrated educational provision, special needs education became an area of particular study by the Foundation. Health and arts education are other examples of areas where a research expertise was developed which then enabled the NFER to win numerous contracts.

In addition to its highly regarded research departments, the NFER had built up much valued information services, serving both the UK education authorities and the European Community, as well as its own Library, which has one of the largest education collections in the country, holding about 25,000 books and subscribing to hundreds of journals. All these services made full use of the bibliographical tools and technology which have now vastly enlarged the scope of reference and information sources that can be accessed world-wide. These research and information activities were facilitated by a structure of dedicated support services, including field research, information technology and statistics services, all of which contribute significantly to the high quality of the NFER's professional output. Dissemination of its research findings – a matter of overriding and repeated concern from the inauguration of the organisation – had been greatly enhanced by the Foundation's co-ownership of a commercially successful publishing company as well as the steady growth of its own expert in-house printing unit. A vital support function is provided to the whole Foundation by its finance and administration section. Smooth running is ensured through well-organised grounds and maintenance services while the high-quality catering services are much appreciated by NFER staff. The two regional offices in Swansea and York, much expanded and diversified, have also evolved their own complementary ethos and established a strong presence in those areas of the country which they particularly serve.

From the middle of 1993, NFER staff were employed on permanent contracts, an unusual situation in this country's research community where many working in comparable establishments are still subject to the uncertainties of contract renewals. The Foundation has had an enviable tradition of investment in the continuing professional development of its staff and in December 1996 was awarded 'Investors in People' status, a recognition of its strong commitment to enhancing the skills of all of its employees. There has always been a strong team spirit engendered among those employed by the Foundation and it also became, over this half century, a 'nursery' for the development of educational research workers who then spread the expertise which they had gained there in their subsequent careers. In accordance with the brief it was given at its founding, the NFER has continued to play a leading role too among the international educational research community.

The support of the educational community in this country, which has valued the NFER's role as a champion of impartial, professional research and analysis of developments, had been a crucial factor in its success. The funding provided by the local authorities and the teacher unions had proved vital both at the Foundation's inception and to its later growth. Local authority officers and advisers had also provided guidance on the issues that needed the attention of the research community. Countless numbers of teachers and children have cooperated in the conduct of the NFER's researches. Central government, recognising the expertise and objective professionalism that resided in the NFER, has awarded the bulk of the contracts which sustained it and which have involved the Foundation in many of the principal educational initiatives of the time.

While this Golden Jubilee history has taken the Foundation's story in detail only up to 1996, the NFER continued to flourish as it entered the 21st century. For those who work at The Mere, the outward and visible sign of its success has been the erection of a spacious new building on the campus, together with large-scale remodelling of the grounds, including the provision of a new vehicle entrance. This work, estimated to cost more than £5 million and scheduled for completion in late 2003, will then provide accommodation for the majority of the 280 staff now working for the NFER. While most of this expansion in staff numbers has taken place in Slough, there has also been a significant increase of personnel in the Northern Office, which has now moved to a new base on the York Science Park. Another significant development was the sale in 2000 of the Foundation's share in the NFER-NELSON Publishing Company to Granada Learning for a sum of around £10 million. The NFER will be continuing its links with the company, nevertheless, and providing it with test development services.

Building on the fine tradition of staff development which the NFER has established, an innovative research training programme has been launched. The PhD Plus, which also incorporates a year's internship, is offered by a consortium comprising the NFER, the Institute of Education, King's College London and the University of Oxford. Intended for those who wish to make a career in research, the Foundation's own staff will also be able to participate in this collaborative postgraduate training scheme. As the Foundation moved with confidence into a new century, significant changes were also effected in its governance with a more streamlined structure put in place. The management of the NFER was transferred from the Council to a smaller Board of Trustees and a new Council of Members was established to ensure that the Foundation conducts its affairs in the best possible manner.

Ultimately, any organisation's success is built upon the vision and drive of those who have overseen and led it, as well as the dedication of those who have served in a variety of roles on its staff – at all levels – over these decades. A particular debt of gratitude is owed to the succession of Honorary Officers, Committee and Board members who have given their time, energies and accumulated experience to the service of the NFER. This history has been able to recount only a small number of these individuals by name. Many Foundation staff testify on leaving its employment – some after substantial periods of service – to the satisfaction that they have found working for an organisation in which they had been able to pursue challenging and meaningful work alongside supportive colleagues and in a pleasant environment. Such professional and personal satisfaction will also have played a significant part in the success achieved by the National Foundation for Educational Research in over 50 years of its flourishing existence.

Appendix 1

The Mere

The Mere, which has been the NFER's headquarters since 1964, was built by the Bentley family. The Foundation has been fortunate to inherit a collection of documents, photographs and items associated with the history of the house, particularly through the generous donation of material relating to the Bentleys gathered by the late Reg Harrison, a local historian. This archive provides a vivid picture of life on the estate of an affluent family from the Victorian era up until its sale in the 1960s.

The Bentleys had been successful publishers who numbered some of the best-known writers of the day among their authors. Charles Dickens was commissioned by them to write *Oliver Twist*, and Wilkie Collins, Marie Corelli and the Victorian Prime Minister, Benjamin Disraeli, were included amongst those whose works appeared under the Bentley imprint. Bentley Publishers were sold to the firm of Macmillan in 1895.

The neo-Tudor mansion, which has a distinctive black and white timbered exterior, described as being in the Shropshire timbered-style (the family came from that county), was built in 1887. It then had 35 rooms and the building included a number of features that were novel for that time, such as internal draught-proof windows – anticipating modern double glazing – and cavity walls, which increased the building's insulation and helped maintain balanced temperatures.

Richard Bentley, the last of the male heirs to live at The Mere, and who died in 1936, took great pride in developing the mansion's grounds, which once covered around five acres. He was President of the Royal Meteorological

Society for 1905–1906 and had a weather station installed in the grounds. A dispute in 1969 between the Foundation and the Meteorological Office as to which of them should pay for repairs to this weather station after it had been vandalised brought to an end a record of daily readings that stretched back to 1873. The former garage to the Bentley estate, bearing an inscription taken from Ovid's *Metamorphosis*, 'In Medio Tutissimus Ibis' ('A middle course is the safest for you to take') is now the only one remaining of a number of outbuildings that once stood on the estate, including a thatched lodge house.

By the time Lucy Bentley, Richard's widow, sold the house and estate in 1961, conditions were much changed for this family which had once been supported in its comfortable life-style at The Mere by a number of servants. The estate was then initially bought by developers and high-rise flats were planned at one time to occupy the former Bentley acres. (Mrs Bentley told a local newspaper that she had wanted at one time to turn the house into a museum for Slough and would have been happy for the whole of the grounds to become public open space [*Slough Observer*, 1960:1].) The local authority also took the opportunity to acquire some of the land, causing complicated site ownership problems in due course when the Foundation bought The Mere as its new headquarters. When it was purchased, the house was still equipped as a grand, domestic dwelling and the contractors who carried out the work of transforming the building into office accommodation had to remove magnificent baths and other exquisite fixtures. (Mrs Bentley said 'I only agreed to the sale because the house would remain as it is. I may even leave some of my furniture here' [*Slough Observer*, 1960:1].) A number of original features, however, do still remain at The Mere from the Bentleys' time, including fireplaces, parquet flooring, decorated plaster ceilings and various fitments. The family claimed descent from a variety of important personalities and their names and heraldic-like devices are displayed on a plaque above the doorway to one of The Mere's principal rooms.

In the light of The Mere's present use, it is interesting to observe that one member of the Bentley family was reputed to be a social reformer who had assisted in organising government inspections of schools and the certification of teachers. Also, that the main bulk of the land purchased by the family on which to build their estate had once been occupied by a local school.

For more information, see *The Mere: A Brief History* by J. L. Griffiths, first published by the NFER in 1987 to mark the centenary of The Mere, and articles by the same author in editions 27, 37 and 39 of the *NFER Newsletter*.

Appendix 2

Directors, Presidents and Officers of the Foundation

Directors

1946–1950	Sir Peter Innes, CBE, MA, DSc
1950–1956	Dr Ben Morris EdB, DSc
1956–1968	Professor William Wall, BA, PhD, DLitt
1968–1971	Dr Stephen Wiseman, MEd, PhD, DSc
1971–March 1972	Dr Douglas Pidgeon, BSc, PhD (Acting Director)
1972–1983	Alfred Yates, CBE, MA, MEd
1983–1993	Dr Clare Burstall, BA, PhD
1993 Oct.–May 1994	Dr Seamus Hegarty BSc, PhD (Acting Director)
1994 June–	Dr Seamus Hegarty BSc, PhD

Presidents of the Foundation

1946–1947	Rt Hon. Ellen Wilkinson, MP
1947–1951	Rt Hon. George Tomlinson, MP
1951–1954	Rt Hon. Florence Horsbrugh, CBE, MP
1954–1956	Rt Hon. Sir David Eccles, MP
1956–1957	Rt Hon. The Viscount Hailsham, QC, MP
1957–1959	Rt Hon. Geoffrey Lloyd, MP
1959–1962	Rt Hon. Sir David Eccles, KCVO, MP
1962–1964	Rt Hon. Sir Edward Boyle, MP
1964–1965	Rt Hon. Michael Stewart, MP
1965–1967	Rt Hon. Anthony Crosland, MP
1967–1968	Rt Hon. Patrick Gordon Walker, MP
1968–1970	Rt Hon. Edward Short, MP

1970–1974	Rt Hon. Margaret Thatcher, MP
1974–1975	Rt Hon. Reginald Prentice, MP
1975–1976	Rt Hon. Frederick Mulley, MP
1976–1979	Rt Hon. Mrs Shirley Williams, MP
1979–1981	Rt Hon. Mark Carlisle, QC, MP
1983–1998	Sir James Hamilton, KCB, MBE

Vice-Presidents

1946–1952	Prof. Sir Fred Clarke, MA, LittD
1948–1971	Prof. Sir Cyril Burt, MA, DSc
1948–1970	Sir Samuel Gurney-Dixon, MA, MD
1948–1964	Sir Frederick Mander, MA, BSc
1953–1955	Sir Godfrey Thomson, PhD, DSc, DCL
1963–1964	Sir Wilfrid Martineau, MC, TD, MA
1964–1986	Sir Ronald Gould, MA, LLD
1967–1980	Sir Francis Hill, CBE, LLM, LittD
1973–1990	Sir Alan Lubbock, MA, FSA
1979–	Sir Edward Britton, CBE, MA, DEd
1983–1989	L. W. K. Brown, CBE, BA
1983–1996	A. W. S. Hutchings, CBE, MA
1990–	Miss J. E .L. Baird, OBE, MA

Chairmen

1946–1949	Prof. Sir Fred Clarke, MA, LittD
1949–1957	Dr G. B. Jeffery, MA, DSc FRS
1958–1963	Sir Wilfrid Martineau, MC, TD, MA
1963–1967	Francis Hill, CBE, LLM, LittD
1967–1973	Sir Alan Lubbock, MA, FSA
1973–1983	A. W. S. Hutchings, CBE, MA
1983–1988	Prof. W. Taylor CBE, DSc, LittD
1988–1990	Sir Wilfred Cockcroft MA, DPhil
1990–1997	Rt Hon. the Lord Peston, BScEcon, DEd
1997–	Mrs N. Harrison, CBE

Vice-Chairmen

1946–1959	W. Griffith, MA
1959–1970	E. L. Britton, MA
1970–1973	A. W. S. Hutchings, MA
1973–1983	L. W. K. Brown, CBE, BA
1983–1985	Mrs S. J. Chaplin (formerly Walpole), MA
1986–1997	Mrs N. Harrison, CBE

(This office ceased to exist in 1997 following a reorganisation of the Board.)

Treasurers

1946–1950	Dr W. P. Alexander, EdB, MA, PhD
1950–1959	E. W. Woodhead, MA, LLB
1959–1962	H. Oldham, MA
1962–1967	S. R. Hutton, BSc
1968–1969	J. M. Bowen, FIMTA, FSAA
1969–1972	F. Stephenson, FIMTA, FRVA
1973–1979	W. S. Page, FIMTA, FRVA
1979–1984	J. A. Barnes, MA, MEd, BSc
1984–1988	P. E. Edwards, MA, MEd
1988–	R. D. C. Bunker, MA

Appendix 3

Acronyms

AEC	Association of Education Committees
AGM	Annual General Meeting
AIDS	Acquired Immune Deficiency Syndrome
APU	Assessment of Performance Unit
AMMA	Assistant Masters and Mistresses Association
BBC	British Broadcasting Corporation
BERA	British Educational Research Association
BP	British Petroleum Company
BRIEF	Briefing Service for Industry on Education
CBAG	Central Bodies Advisory Group
CBE	Commander of the Order of the British Empire
CERI	Centre for Educational Research and Innovation
CIDREE	Consortium of Institutions for Development and Research in Education in Europe
CITE	Centre for the Evaluation of Information Technology in Education
CLEA	Council of Local Education Authorities
CLASP	Consortium of Local Authorities Special Programme
CSE	Certificate of Secondary Education
CSG	Curriculum Study Group
DfEE	Department for Education and Employment
DES	Department of Education and Science
EMIE	Education Management Information Exchange
EPIC	Education Policy Information Centre (later EPIC Europe), a part of the European Community's EURYDICE education information network
ESRC	Economic and Social Research Council
EUDISED	European Documentation and Information System in Education
EURYDICE	This is not an acronym but is the name chosen for this European education information network. See also EPIC.

IEA	International Association for the Evaluation of Educational Achievement
GCSE	General Certificate of Secondary Education
HMI	Her (or His) Majesty's Inspectorate (or Inspector) of Schools
HIV	Human Immunodeficiency Virus
INSET	In-service education and training
i.t.a.	Initial teaching alphabet
LAPP	Lower Attaining Pupils Programme
LEA	Local Education Authority
LEASIB	Local Education Authorities and Schools Item Bank
LDTC	London Day Training College
LMS	Local Management of Schools
MBE	Member of the Order of the British Empire
MIER	More Interest in Educational Research
MSC	Manpower Services Commission
MSU	Monitoring Services Unit
NCC	National Curriculum Council
NFER	National Foundation for Educational Research
NUT	National Union of Teachers
NVQ	National Vocational Qualification
OBE	Officer of the Order of the British Empire
OECD	Organisation for Economic Co-operation and Development
QUASE	Quantitative Analysis for Self-Evaluation
SATs	Standard Assessment Tasks
SCAA	School Curriculum and Assessment Authority
SCRE	Scottish Council for Research in Education
SCU	School Coordinating Unit
SCYA	Sefydliad Cenedlaethol er Ymchwil i Addysg (the Welsh version of the NFER's name)
SEAC	School Examinations and Assessment Council
TGAT	Task Group on Assessment and Testing
TIMSS	Third International Mathematics and Science Study
TVEI	Technical and Vocational Education Initiative
UNESCO	United Nations Educational, Scientific and Cultural Organization
USA	United States of America
USSR	Union of Soviet Socialist Republics

Appendix 4

Chart of Key Events

1931   The Carnegie Corporation funds the International Examinations Enquiry, in which UK and European researchers take part, to check the reliability and validity of formal public examinations.

1932   The London Day Training College is transformed into the University of London Institute of Education. A key objective for the new Institute is the creation of a 'Bureau of Educational Enquiries and Research'.

1943   The first meeting of the 'Advisory Council of the Educational Research Fund', representing all the main interests concerned with education in England and Wales, takes place in January.

1944   The Education Act passed in Parliament includes powers for the Ministry of Education and the LEAs to fund research on educational provision. More than £6,300 is raised to support this new research organisation. Its first paid employee is taken on and work begins on research projects.

1945   A conference meets in December to set up a National Foundation for Educational Research in England and Wales with the Minister of Education being invited to become its President. An Interim Executive and Welsh Committee are appointed.

1946   The Association of Education Committees recommends that all LEAs support this new research body.

1947   From 1 April, the NFER becomes a self-governing body. The first Director of the Foundation, Sir Peter Innes, is appointed. The offices at 79 Wimpole Street in London are bought. The Ministry of Education gives its first grant of £3,500 to the Foundation.

1948   Following the decision of the Privy Council not to recommend that a Royal Charter be granted, a Constitution is prepared for the Foundation. Three NFER Vice-Presidents are appointed.

1949   A Tests Division is set up in the Foundation and a Test Import Agency is later formed. The NFER's principal founder, Sir Fred Clarke, retires from the post of Chairman of the Executive Committee.

1950   The first two NFER publications appear. The Foundation's second Director, Ben Morris, is appointed.

1952   Doubling of the level of subscriptions for membership of the Foundation. Research is undertaken at this time into secondary school entrance examinations.

1953   A Statement of Policy is adopted.

1956   Professor William Wall is appointed as Director.

1958   *Educational Research*, the Foundation's journal, is launched.

1963   Appointment of the first Deputy Director, Douglas Pidgeon. The Foundation's Test Services and Test Agency grow significantly and 2.5 million copies of the Foundation's own tests are sold.

1964   The Foundation's main office moves to The Mere in Slough. Research into comprehensive schools begins in the 1960s, a decade of rapid growth for the NFER.

1967   The Foundation becomes an incorporated, charitable body. Henceforth, the NFER draws its income from pooled funds rather than directly from each separate local authority. The Foundation sets up an Education and Training Scheme to assist its staff to follow higher and further education courses.

1968   Appointment of Dr Stephen Wiseman as Director. The first computer is installed.

1969   The Test Agency is transformed into the NFER Publishing Company and moves to Windsor.

1971   The Foundation's 25th anniversary. The Director, Dr Wiseman, dies in post in July. He is succeeded by Alfred Yates, who writes a personal account of the Foundation's history up to the time of its Silver Jubilee.

1972   The Wimpole Street premises are sold. A permanent extension to The Mere (the Research Block) is completed. Formation of the NFER Social Club.

1973   Publication of the NFER's first Register of Current Educational Research and Development.

1974   NFER Liaison Officers are appointed in the LEAs.

1977   The first of the Assessment of Performance Unit (APU) teams is set up. The NFER Publishing Company moves to Darville House in Windsor. During 1977/78, the Foundation's income exceeds £1 million for the first time with an average of 112 staff being employed.

1978   The establishment in Wales of the first of the Foundation's regional offices.

1981   The NFER-NELSON Publishing Company, jointly owned by the Foundation and Thomas Nelson & Sons Ltd., is formed. The government's principal Education Minister ceases to hold the honorary post of NFER President.

1983   The Foundation's sixth Director, Dr Clare Burstall, assumes office. A new departmental structure is introduced.

1984/85 A new era of educational evaluation begins with major contracts (LAPP and TVEI) secured from the DES and MSC.

1986   The Foundation's Northern Office is set up at the University of York. Funding from industry is attracted for the first time to set up an information service named BRIEF.

1987   The centenary of the building of The Mere, the NFER's HQ, is celebrated. Exceptional storms destroy mature trees in the surrounding grounds.

1988   The NFER becomes heavily involved in the development of new National Curriculum assessment techniques following the Education Reform Act 1988.

1989   *TOPIC*, a magazine developed with NFER-NELSON for classroom practitioners, is launched. NFER Enterprises, the short-lived commercial company, is set up.

1990   Joyce Baird is appointed as the first woman Vice-President. The first Staff Conference Day is organised.

1993   Open-ended employment contracts are given to all those on the NFER's permanent research staff.

1994   After a period as Acting Director, Dr Seamus Hegarty is appointed to lead the Foundation.

1996   The NFER celebrates its Golden Jubilee. A residential conference hosted by the Foundation to examine the role of educational research brings together leading researchers from around the world. The NFER is awarded 'Investors in People' status.

References

ALDRICH, R. (2002). *The Institute of Education 1902–2002: A Centenary History*. London: Institute of Education University of London.

ALDRICH R., COOK, D. and WATSON, D. (2000). *Education and Employment: The DfEE and its Place in History*. London: Bedford Way Papers, University of London Institute of Education.

BARBER, M. (1996). *The National Curriculum: A Study in Policy*. Keele: Keele University Press.

BARNETT C. (2001). *The Verdict of Peace: Britain Between Her Yesterday and the Future*. London: Macmillan.

BLACKWELL, A.M. (1950). *A List of Researchers in Education and Educational Psychology Presented for Higher Degrees in the Universities of the United Kingdom, Northern Ireland, and the Irish Republic from 1918–1948*. London: Newnes Educational Publishing Co.

CARNEGIE CORPORATION OF NEW YORK. The records covering the period when a grant was made to what became the NFER are located at the Columbia Rare Book and Manuscript Library, Columbia University, New York, USA.

CLARKE, F. (n.d.). *The Sir Fred Clarke Papers*. Library, Institute of Education, University of London. The papers also include documentation from the period when other Directors of the Institute of Education were members of the Foundation's Board.

COOPER, J.D. (1993). 'The origins of the National Children's Bureau.' In: PUGH, G. (Ed) *30 Years of Change for Children*. London: National Children's Bureau.

CRAIGIE J. (1972). *The Scottish Council for Research in Education 1928–1972*. Edinburgh: Scottish Council for Research Education.

CURTIS, S. and BOULTWOOD, M.E.A. (1965). *A Short History of Educational Ideas*. Fourth edn. London: University Tutorial Press.

DAVIE, R. (1993). 'The impact of the National Child Development Study.' In: PUGH, G. (Ed) *30 Years of Change for Children*. London: National Children's Bureau.

DEAN, M. (1987). 'Standing the test of time: comparison of the old 11+ exam and new proposed tests', *Education Guardian*, 13 October, 13.

DIXON, C. W. (1986). *The Institute: A Personal Account of the History of the University of London Institute of Education 1932–72*. London: University of London Institute of Education.

DUNSDON, M.I. (1952). *The Educability of Cerebral Palsied Children*. London: Newnes Educational Publishing Co.

FOXMAN, D., HUTCHINSON, D. and BLOOMFIELD, B. (1991). *The APU Experience 1977–1990*. London: School Examinations and Assessment Council.

GRAHAM, D. with TYTLER, D. (1993). *A Lesson For Us All: The Making of the National Curriculum*. London: Routledge.

GREAT BRITAIN. BOARD OF TRADE (1967). *Memorandum and Articles of Association of the National Foundation for Educational Research*. London: HMSO.

GREAT BRITAIN. PARLIAMENT. HOUSE OF COMMONS (1903). *Papers Relating to the Resignation of the Director of Special Enquiries and Reports* (Cm.1602). London: HMSO. Cited in TAYLOR, W. (Ed) (1973). *Research Perspectives in Education*. London: Routledge & Kegan Paul.

GRIFFITHS, J.L. (1987 and later editions). *The Mere: A Brief History*. Slough: NFER.

HARTOG, P. and RHODES, E.C. (1936). *An Examination of Examinations*. Second edn. London: Macmillan.

HEGARTY, S. (1996). 'A half-century of educational research', *Educational Research*, **38**, 3, 243–57.

HEGARTY, S. (Ed) (1997). *The Role of Research in Mature Education Systems: Proceedings of the NFER International Jubilee Conference, Oakley Court, Windsor, 2-4 December 1996*. Slough: NFER.

HIGHFIELD, M. and PINSENT, A. (1952) *A Survey of Rewards and Punishments in Schools* (A Report by the National Foundation for Educational Research in England and Wales, No. 3). London: Newnes Educational Publishing Co.

KOGAN, M. (1978). *The Politics of Educational Change*. Manchester: Manchester University Press.

LINACRE, J. (1995). 'Bruce Choppin: Visionary', *Rasch Measurement Transactions*, **8**, 4, 394.

MACLURE, S. (2000). *The Inspectors' Calling: HMI and The Shaping of Educational Policy 1945–1992*. London: Hodder and Stoughton.

MITCHELL, F.W. (1967). *Sir Fred Clarke: Master-teacher, 1880–1952*. London: Longmans.

MORGAN, G.A.V. (1953). 'The Test Import Agency', *NFER Bulletin*, **1**, March, 25.

MORRIS, B.S. (1952). 'The National Foundation for Educational Research in England and Wales', *British Journal of Educational Studies*, **1**, 1, 33–8.

MORRIS, J.M. (1959). *Reading in the Primary School: An Investigation into Standards of Reading and their Association with Primary School Characteristics*. London: Newnes Educational Publishing Co.

MORRIS, J.M. (1966). *Standards and Progress in Reading*. Slough: NFER.

MORRIS, J.M. (1996). 'A reading researcher looks back and forward with the NFER', *NFER Newsletter*, **37**, 12–15.

MORRIS, J.M. (2002a). 'Joyce Morris shares her life for literacy. Part 1: Background to a vocation', *History of Reading News*, **25**, spring, 3–4, 6.

MORRIS, J.M. (2002b). 'Joyce Morris shares her life for literacy. Part 2: Serving a good cause', *History of Reading News*, **26**, fall, 1–2, 5–7.

MURPHY, R. and BROADFOOT, P. (1995). *Effective Assessment and the Improvement of Education – A Tribute to Desmond Nuttall*. London: Falmer.

NATIONAL FOUNDATION FOR EDUCATIONAL RESEARCH (1947–2002). *Annual Reports of The National Foundation for Educational Research*. London and Slough: NFER.

NATIONAL FOUNDATION FOR EDUCATIONAL RESEARCH (1953). *Statement of Policy*. London: NFER.

NATIONAL FOUNDATION FOR EDUCATIONAL RESEARCH (1970). *Newsletter*, Nos. 13–15, October–December.

NATIONAL FOUNDATION FOR EDUCATIONAL RESEARCH (1972). 'A nest in the woods', *NFER Newsletter*, 8, November.

NATIONAL FOUNDATION FOR EDUCATIONAL RESEARCH (1977–). Social Club Minutes. Slough: NFER (unpublished).

NEWSAM, P. (2002). Lord Alexander Lecture to ConfEd Conference, London, 13 July.

POLLARD, M. (1971). 'Sacred Cows 3: The Researchers', *Education and Training*, May, pp.158–9,166.

PUGH, G. (Ed) (1993). *30 Years of Change for Children*. London: National Children's Bureau.

PYKE, N. (1996). 'Putting more sparkle into a dull image' (Research Focus), *Times Educ. Suppl.*, 6 December, 15.

SAINSBURY, M. (Ed) (1996). *SATs: The Inside Story: The Development of the First National Assessments for Seven-year-olds, 1989–1995*. Slough: NFER.

SLOUGH OBSERVER (1960). 'Offices and houses at The Mere: parkland lost to Slough', *Slough Observer*, **4028**, 12 August, 1.

SUMNER, R. (1975). *Tests of Attainment in Mathematics: Monitoring Feasibility Study*. Slough: NFER.

SUMNER, R. (1996). 'The Gas Man', *NFER Newsletter*, **37**, April, 24–6.

TAYLOR, T. (1995). 'Movers and Shakers: high politics and the origins of the National Curriculum', *The Curriculum Journal*, **6**, 2, 160–84.

TAYLOR, W. (Ed) (1973). *Research Perspectives in Education*. London: Routledge & Kegan Paul.

THOMSON, G. (1953). 'Sir Godfrey Thomson's address to the Sixth Annual Meeting of Council', *NFER Bulletin*, 2, November, 11.

WATTS, A. F and SLATER, P. (1950). *The Allocation of Primary School Leavers to Courses of Secondary Education: First Interim Report*. London: Newnes Educational Publishing Co.

WILLIAMS, B. (1994). *Education With Its Eyes Open: A Biography of Dr. K.S. Cunningham*. Victoria: The Australian Council for Educational Research Ltd.

YATES, A. (1953). 'The Foundation's approach to primary school studies', *NFER Bulletin*, 2, November, 26.

YATES, A. (1971). *The First Twenty-five Years: A Review of the NFER 1946–1971*. Slough: NFER.

YATES, A. (1977). 'Does research make a difference?' Paper delivered at the NFER Annual Members' Conference, 8 December. Slough: NFER.

YATES, A. (1996). 'A few random reminiscences…', *NFER Newsletter*, 37, 10.

Names Index

Page numbers in **bold** indicate a photograph and those in *italic* indicate a footnote.

Subject Index

Page numbers in **bold** indicate a photograph and those in *italic* indicate a footnote.